TABLE OF CONTENTS

Internet Basics for Beginners

Internet Basics for Beginners

How To Send E-Mails and Surf the Net With Ease

By Shaun Fawcett, M.B.A.

Eliminate Techie-Talk Forever!

Have you ever been turned-off by techno-speak and wished for easy to understand point-and-click information so you can quickly and easily send e-mails and surf the Net?

If so, this book is your answer …

eBook Solutions.net

Saving You Time and Money

Library and Archives Canada Cataloguing in Publication

Fawcett, Shaun, 1949-
Internet basics for beginners: how to send e-mails and surf the net with ease / Shaun Fawcett.

Includes bibliographical references and index.

ISBN: 978-0-9781700-3-5

1. Internet. 2. Electronic mail systems. 3. Internet searching. I. Title.

TK5105.875.I57F388 2007 004.67'8 C2007-903676-7

Final Draft Publications
1501 Notre-Dame West, Suite No. 5
Montreal QC, Canada H3C 1L2

http://www.WritingHelpTools.com

Disclaimer

This book was written as a guide only, and does not claim to be the final definitive word on any of the subjects covered. The statements made and opinions expressed are the personal observations and assessments of the author based on his own experiences and were not intended to prejudice any party. There may be errors or omissions in this guide. As such, the author or publisher does not accept any liability or responsibility for any loss or damage that may have been caused, or alleged to have been caused, through use of the information contained in this manual. Errors or omissions will be corrected in future editions, provided the publisher receives written notification of such.

To Deena

A good friend.

PREFACE

A lot of things have happened with respect to the Internet since I wrote my first book for Internet beginners back in 2000. What was then a scary proposition to be avoided by many people, has since become a part of everyday life at home, at work and at school. Sending and receiving e-mails and surfing the Net are now part of the daily routine for most people in the developed world.

Nevertheless, there are still a few holdouts or "late adopters" when it comes to embracing the Internet. Whatever the reasons, perhaps 20% or more of adults in developed countries are still not fully online.

So, I have decided to write this book in the same spirit as my original Internet beginners book; that is, to reach out to those who have been marginalized from the Net, for whatever reason, and give them a simple tool to help them become functional online.

A True How-To Book

The thing that really got me excited about this particular project is that I can now take advantage of relatively recent new technology to produce a more user-friendly product to which most beginners should be able to easily relate.

As a result, I have been able to include more than 100 real-life screen shots in this book. In addition, as a bonus I have created a series of point-and-click video tutorials that I have posted online for the use of anyone who has purchased this book. With these technical innovations I believe that this book, combined with the complementary video tutorials, is the most hands-on "how to" of all of my how-to books to-date.

In fact, while creating this book, I have tried to make a point of answering all of the typical "how-to" questions that I believe are asked by the average Internet beginner with respect to sending and receiving e-mails and surfing the Net. Indeed, a quick look at the Table of Contents reveals more than 30 occurrences of the terms "how" and "how to".

Get Access To the Video Tutorials

If you purchased this book and you want to get direct online access to the video tutorials please send an e-mail to the following address:
videos35@writinghelptools.com

In that e-mail you MUST include the following information: your full name, full telephone number, and your primary e-mail address. Also indicate the date you purchased the book, the business you purchased it from, as well as the Order Number or Transaction Number you received from the vendor.

Access info will be sent to you normally within 24 hours of receiving your e-mail.

INTRODUCTION

Opening Notes

Back in the year 2000 I wrote another book for Internet beginners. That one was partly inspired by watching my own Father's experience getting online and learning how to send e-mails and surf the Net while he was in his mid-seventies. That was back in the early days of the Internet; before it was a routine daily communications tool for the majority of average people.

In those days the Internet was relatively new and the majority of regular people were not yet online. Most of the "early adopters" were "techie types" and business people who had started using the Net in their day-to-day business and personal lives. A lot has changed since then, with an estimated 75%+ people in North America now online in one way or another.

A problem that existed in those early days, a scant half-dozen years ago, was that many of the computer programs that were available for people to send/receive e-mails and surf the Internet were still evolving and not necessarily all that "user friendly" -- at least for beginners.

Novelty Of the Net Is Wearing Off

At that time there was still a lot of fear-creating "mystique" about the relatively new phenomenon, the World Wide Web. This situation was exacerbated since "techie types" tended to dominate the provision of information on how to use the technology, thus making it difficult for the average person to grasp how to use it in their daily lives.

Because of that, my first book on the subject reached out to those people who were still marginalized from the Net due to their fear of technology and the prevalence of "techno babble" to further confuse and alienate them. That's why that first book was titled *Internet Basics without fear! Quick-Start Guide for Becoming Internet-Friendly In Just A Few Easy Steps.* For absolute clarity as to the target market, the one-liner slogan on the cover read; *A Non-Technical Book for Non-Technical People.*

In fact almost one-third of that book was dedicated to the subject of the "fear of technology" that was preventing many people from going online. I shared there how I had also once experienced many of those same fears, and how I had managed to overcome them. The rest of that book focused on the basics of getting online and performing the essentials of sending/receiving e-mails and surfing the Net.

As it turned out there was indeed a market for that Internet beginners book; it sold more than 4,500 copies over a couple of years. That's not a bad sales figure since I self-published the book and managed to generate that level of sales on a marketing budget close to zero. As recent as last week I receive d a phone call from someone who wanted to buy their own copy to replace the one they had borrowed from the library.

My Mother Made Me Do It

Now, almost seven years later I am writing this follow-up book which was largely inspired by watching my Mother get Internet capable over the past few years. In fact, *this is the book that I should have written for my Mother* about three or four years ago! It would have been a big help to her at the time. "Sorry Mom, but I guess I needed to see you go through the experience first so that I would know what to cover in this book!" I guess it's true that a mother's work is never done!

Following are what I believe to be the major improvements and changes in approach that I have included in this new guide for Internet beginners:

- There is much less emphasis in this book on the "fear of technology" aspect since the situation has changed significantly over the past six years. The "mystique" that once surrounded the Internet is gone, and so has much of the fear that went with it. And, most of the major software tools that people use to work/access the Net with are much more intuitive and user-friendly than before.

- The focus of this book is on the actual point-and-click practical "how-to" aspects of performing the basic online tasks related to sending/receiving e-mails and surfing online. Accordingly, extensive use has been made of actual real-life "screen shots" of what people will actually see on their own computer screens.

My Internet Background

My name is Shaun Fawcett. I am a Canadian-based writer, publisher, business consultant, and journalist. Over the past 30 years I have worked in a variety of professional capacities in both the private and public sectors. I earned my M.B.A. in 1996 through the University of Ottawa's Executive MBA Program. Below are some experiences that I believe qualify me to write this guide for Internet beginners.

I first came online in 1994 when I was working on my M.B.A. at Ottawa U. As I stated earlier, I wrote and self-published my first book *Internet Basics without fear!* back in 2000. Shortly after that, I set up my first writing help website, www.WritingHelp-Central.com. My idea at the time was to create a small portal site that offered free writing help content and provided links to the writing related products of others.

Since then, that WritingHelp-Central website has grown significantly. As I write this, that site contains more than 200 pages and over 175,000 words of free writing-help-related information on such topics as: letter writing, resume/c.v. writing, essay writing, book writing, business writing, copy writing, and much more. That website currently receives more than 3 million visits per year, making it one of the most visited websites of its type.

In parallel with maintaining that free content writing help website; since 2001 I have written and published ten (10) how-to books on various aspects of writing, from letter writing to book writing. Those books can be seen at my Writing Help Tools website: http://writinghelptools.com

Because I have been making my entire living online since 2002, almost every day of my life for the past seven years has been spent surfing the Net and sending/receiving e-mails as I develop my products and run my online businesses. It is the knowledge and experience that I have gained online as a daily "hands-on user" that I believe qualifies me to pen this guide for Internet beginners.

Why I Wrote This Book

As I mentioned earlier, watching my Mother stumble her way to become Internet-friendly by trial and error over the past few years got me thinking that it was time to update my 2000 book *Internet Basics with fear!* Actually, Mom did say that the original book did help her at times along the way. But let's face it; a lot of that book has been out-of-date for the past five years, at least. So, it is definitely time for an update.

Also, I realized that as the result of a couple of important breakthroughs in technology in recent years, I would be able to present my how-to information to readers in a much more accessible and user-friendly way.

I am referring in particular here to two pieces of software that I have acquired over the last couple of years. One allows me to easily capture real-life, real-time screen shots of anything that appears on my screen, and then quickly and easily edit and manipulate those images as I choose for presentation purposes in a book such as this. The other software program allows me to create live action video screen captures of anything that I do on my screen and then save those online for viewing later by my readers.

Clearly, through the use of both words and images this book communicates my "how-to" message better than the previous one did.

Finally, even though the Internet is now a household word throughout the developed world there is still a significant segment of the population that is not yet online. I believe that the barriers that have kept these people offline to-date are beginning to crumble and within a few years will be largely eradicated in the developed countries. I refer here to such barriers as: high price, lack of access, and fear of technology.

This book has been written so that when those final reluctant hold-outs do eventually come online they will have a simple user-friendly point-and-click guide to familiarize them with the essential basics of sending/receiving e-mails and surfing the Net.

Who This Book Is For

This book is for the 20% or so of people in developed countries who still have not yet used the Internet, or who have may have only sampled it in passing.

It is also for the other 5% to 10% of people in those countries who use the Internet but are not defined as regular users and may still have some basics to learn. These are people who sign onto the Internet once or twice a week but spend only a couple of hours or less online and feel unsure of what they are doing.

Finally, this guide is also for the "technophobes" from all walks of life, especially: seniors, homemakers, and self-employed business people. These people need a simple way to learn the basic functions of the Internet and to find out how it can be used as a tool to improve the quality and productivity of their daily lives.

Who This Book Is NOT For

This book is NOT FOR those ordinary people who are already knowledgeable, experienced, and reasonably adept Internet users; although some of those folks would probably find it to be a useful reference on a number of topics.

And, this book is definitely NOT FOR the more extreme Internet users who spend a good part of their lives connected to cyberspace. These people are also affectionately known by a number of terms including: techies, propeller-heads, cyber-surfers, geeks, cyber-heads, web-waifs, among others similar descriptors. By definition, this guide would not be needed by any of those people.

Believe it or not, in spite of many warnings to the contrary, a few techies actually purchased my first Internet beginners book back in 2001. Even though it was clearly aimed at Internet beginners, a couple of those folks actually complained that it was too simplistic!

So, if you are a knowledgeable and experienced Internet user and/or a techie, this book IS NOT for you.

WHAT YOU NEED TO KNOW FIRST

As I stated earlier, the whole idea behind this guide is to answer all of the basic questions that a beginner like my Mom had when she first came online and needed to know the basics to send e-mails and surf the Net.

Most of these questions were directly related to sending e-mails and/or surfing the Web However, it turns out that to be able to perform some of the basics of e-mailing and online surfing, there are a few things that one needs to know about the basic operation of a PC (personal computer) and its operating system (e.g. MS-Windows).

Don't worry, you don't need to become a techie! Nevertheless, there are a few simple definitions and basic concepts that you need to understand if you want to be able to be productive when sending/receiving e-mails and surfing the Net.

Essential Basic Definitions

The following terms and topics are ones that I realized while working with my Mom and other beginners were important for people to understand BEFORE they could successfully send/receive e-mails and perform the basics of surfing the Net.

Key Terms To Know

Hard Drive

This is the permanent file storage device on your computer to which files are copied and saved; and where you later retrieve them from when you need them. Your computer's hard drive is often referred to as your C-drive.

Window

This is the generic term used to describe the entire active working/viewing area that you see in front of you on your computer screen; no matter what software program you are using. The "Active Window" is the window that you are currently viewing. That is, if you have multiple windows open at the same time, the Active Window is the one that is currently "on top".

Desktop

Your Desktop is the opening window/screen that you see when your computer operating system is first started up. Typically, your Desktop window will contain a number of small Icons that you can click on to perform various functions. For example, the following is the Desktop window of my computer as I write this.

Figure 1.1 Typical Desktop Window

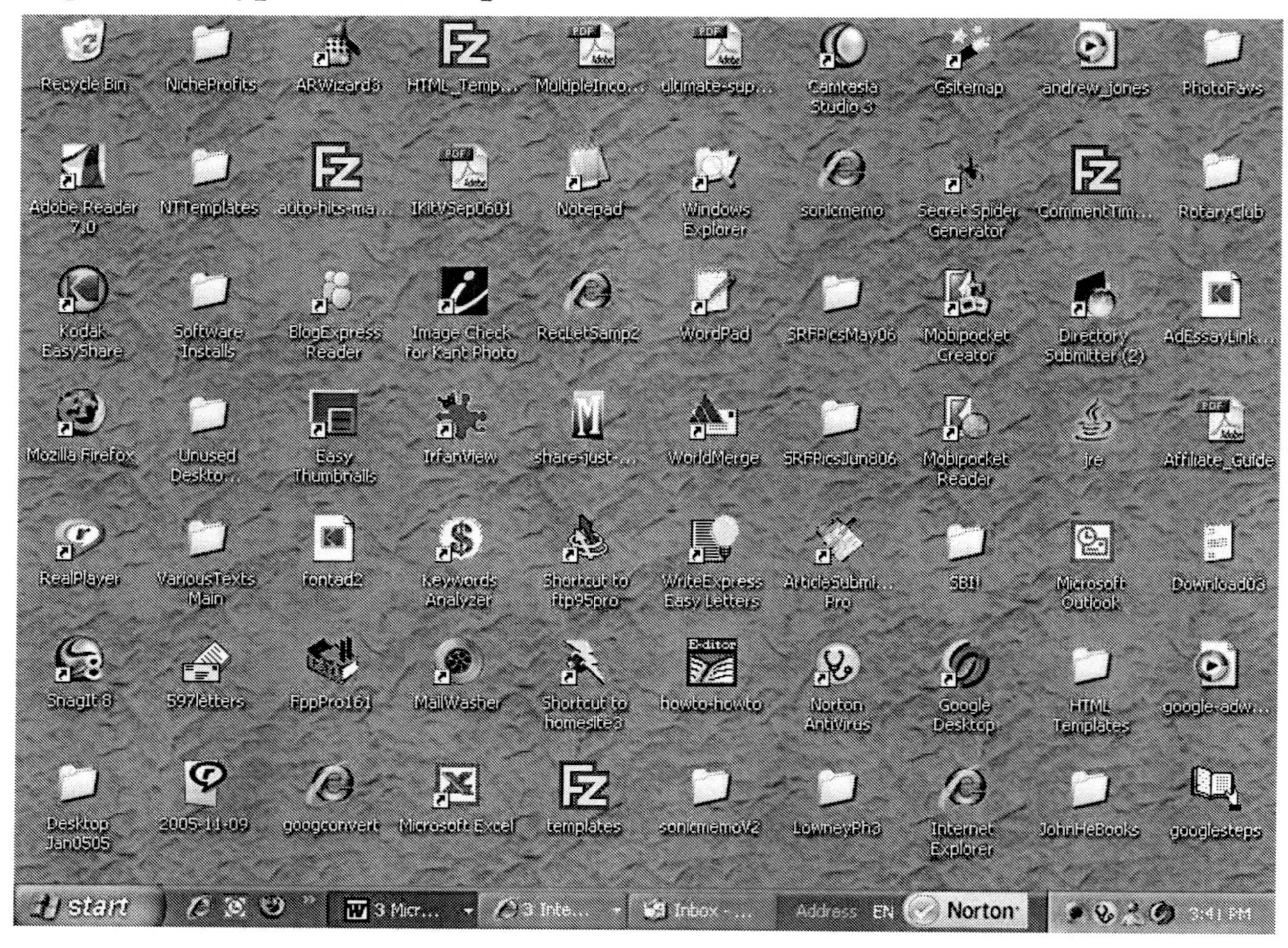

Although it is normally referred to as the Desktop, you can also think of it as the "Dashboard" of your computer; just like the one in your car.

When your Desktop window is your active window, it gives you one-click direct entry access to most of the functions on your computer from one place. Just like with the Dashboard on your car, when you are looking at the Desktop of your PC you are in the best position to control what goes on.

Browser

A Browser is the software program that you use when you are connected to the Internet. The most popular Web browser program is MS-Internet Explorer (IE), which is used by about 85% of all people connected to the Net. The second most popular is currently Mozilla Firefox, which is used by about 7% of Web users at this time. Firefox tends to be used mostly by techies and more advanced Web users. Because IE is so widespread, it is the main browser I use for screen shots in this guide.

Server

A Server is a larger computer that links your computer with the World Wide Web. Your Internet Service Provider (ISP) would typically have hundreds of servers managing the thousands of users that use that company to link to the Internet.

ISP: Web/Mail Host

An Internet Service Provider (ISP) is simply the company that you use to connect you to the Internet. For example, I pay Bell Canada's Business Service to supply and manage my Internet connection. Thus, Bell Canada is my ISP.

In addition to providing you with a connection to the Internet so you can surf the Web, your ISP will also provide you with an e-mail account(s) so that you can send/receive e-mails. The name of your ISP will always be embedded in your e-mail address. For example, my e-mail addresses with Bell looks like: myaddress@bellnet.ca, where "myaddress" may vary, but the "@bellnet.ca" is always a fixed part of my address.

Even though most people have a paid ISP that supplies e-mail accounts as part of the service, many folks choose to use free e-mail services such as hotmail, yahoo mail, google mail, etc. These services provide unlimited free webmail accounts and other free services, and are popular among casual (i.e. non-business) users. The primary reason why these free webmail services are so popular is that one can access one's e-mail account for free from anywhere in the world, as long as one has access to the Internet. So, if all you want to do online is check your e-mail from time-to-time, you don't need to pay an ISP to provide you with Internet access. Instead you can use an Internet connection provided for free at work, school, through a friend, or otherwise.

Cursor

The Cursor is the little symbol that you see on the screen whenever you move the mouse around or when you single-click on your mouse. A lot of beginners tend to get confused by the cursor and just how it works. The graphic symbol used most often for the cursor is a small arrowhead pointer as follows:

Basically, as you move the mouse around with your hand, the pointer moves around your screen and shows you the relative position of the cursor on the screen. When the pointer reaches the place where you want to perform a particular task, you click on the left-button and the action will be initiated at that exact spot. Sometimes you need to single-click your left mouse button, while other times you double-click the left button twice, depending on what the situation requires.

For example; in order to type this particular sentence I moved my pointer (i.e. cursor) to the position just to the left of the position where you see the letter "F" in the word "For" at the beginning of this sentence. I then left-clicked once on my mouse and typed-in the rest of the sentence using my keyboard. In most programs, once you have positioned the cursor by clicking on it, it will begin blinking so you can easily spot it.

Hyperlinks

These are the "live" or "clickable" links that you will see in e-mails and on webpages. When you click on one you will be taken instantly to another location either on the same website or to another website. Hyperlinks are almost always light blue and underlined, and look like this: www.writinghelptools.com. When you pass your mouse over top of a live/active hyperlink a small hand will appear, indicating it is clickable.

Internet

In simple non-technical terms, the Internet, or Net, is a series of thousands of interconnected computer networks, each with a single point of access that connects the user to an electronic information system that spans the entire planet. You don't need to know how the Net works to use it and benefit from it.

Web Versus Net

The term Web is short for World Wide Web (i.e. www). The term Net is short for the term Internet. Although there are some technical differences between these two, you don't need to know what those are to surf the Net and send/receive e-mails. So, the terms Web and Net will be used interchangeably throughout this book.

Default

In the computer world the term "default" means "initial" or "automatic" setting. This may seem obvious to some people, but not everyone knows what the term "default" means in the context of software. So, when I refer to "default setting(s)" I am talking about the very first or automatic manufacturer settings that are in place when you install a piece of software, BEFORE you change anything.

Essential Basic Concepts

As with the basic definitions covered above, there are a few basic concepts about using a PC that are important to understand if you want to be able to productively send and receive e-mails and surf the Web. If you have worked with a PC for any period of time you may already understand these concepts and how to apply them; in which case you can move on to the next section of this guide.

The three basic operations that you need to understand and master to effectively send/receive e-mails and surf the Net are:

1. How To Use the Virtual Clipboard
2. How To Copy and Paste
3. How To Cut and Paste

Once you know how to perform these operations, sending/receiving e-mails and surfing the Net will be a piece of cake.

Using the Virtual Clipboard

The Clipboard is a special place in your computer's memory that is managed by your computer's operating system, where you can temporarily store text and data for later use while you are working. You must have a basic understanding of how this Virtual Clipboard works if you are going to be able to successfully Cut and Paste and/or Copy and Paste text and data.

An important point about the Clipboard that many people often don't understand at first is that it is managed by your computer's overall operating system and is therefore available to access from ANY program that you may be working with.

For example, say you Copy something (e.g. text, data, image) while you are in your word processing program (e.g. MS-Word). That copied info is saved straight onto the virtual Clipboard and stays there indefinitely, or until you replace it with something else.

Now, say that you need that same info that you just copied onto the Clipboard (via MS-Word) in another program, such as your e-mail program. No problem, that's easy. Just open your e-mail program and go into Compose Mode and place your cursor in the exact position where you would like that text pasted. Then, right-click on your mouse and the edit options menu will be displayed, as follows:

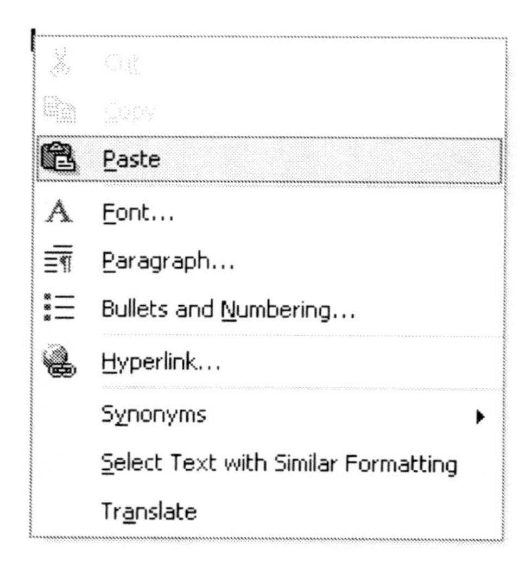

You will notice that the Paste icon is enabled. That's because there is something currently active on your Clipboard (i.e. the text that you just pasted there while in your word processing program). Just click on Paste and the info will be copied from the Clipboard to the exact place you indicated with your cursor.

This Paste from the Clipboard function works in ANY application that you happen to be in, so it is an extremely useful function; one that you will use often when sending and receiving e-mails and surfing the Web.

How To Copy and Paste

I have found that a lot of beginners have trouble with this concept at first. If you don't understand how this works you will not be able to fully benefit from the experience of sending/receiving e-mails and surfing the Net.

The ability to Copy and Paste is especially useful when you are replying to e-mails or when you find some text or graphics on a webpage that you would like to copy into one of your own documents.

You Copy and Paste whenever you want to take a duplicate copy of some text and then insert or paste that copy into another place.

1. Before copying the text, you first have to highlight it. To do this, place the cursor at one end of the text that you want to copy.

2. Second, you left lick on your mouse button and HOLD the button down.

3. With the mouse button STILL depressed, drag (i.e. move or slide) the mouse across the text you want to copy. It will then be highlighted with a black background.

4. When you reach the end point of the text that you want to copy, release the mouse button that you have been holding down. You will see that the text remains highlighted in black. This tells the program that you are working with that you want to perform an operation on that text that you just highlighted.

Here's a sample sentence with text that I want to highlight and copy.

5. Now that the text is highlighted, you can copy it by right-clicking on a portion of the highlighted text and choosing the Copy function from the menu that appears, as follows:

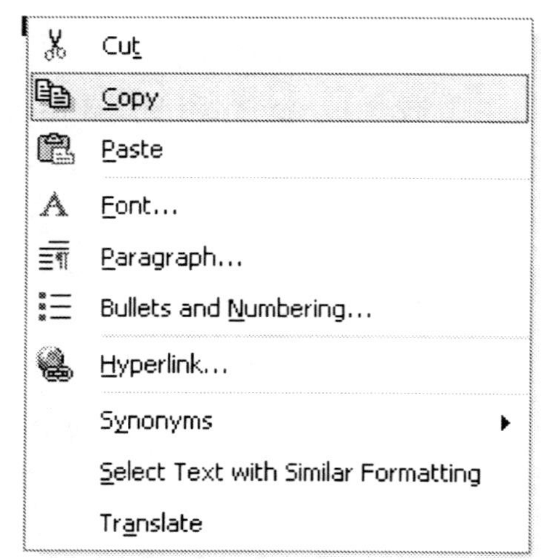

6. Left-click on the Copy item that is highlighted on the menu. That will save a copy of the text that you have just copied to the virtual Clipboard from which you can later access it and use it whenever, wherever you like.

7. Now that you have Copied the text to the Clipboard, you will want to paste it wherever else you want it to appear in your document. To do that, go to the place in your document where you want to insert the copied text. For example, to Paste the text we just copied above to directly below the next paragraph, you simply position your cursor at the exact point where you want the text to be inserted.

8. Then, right-click at that point to display the edit options menu, as follows:

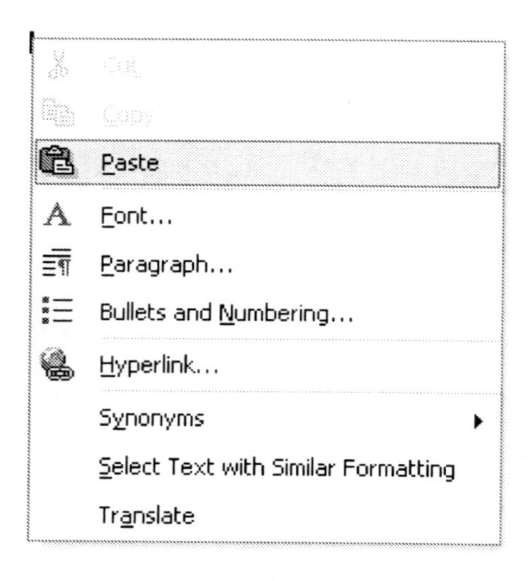

9. Once you have positioned the cursor in the exact position in your document where you want the text to be inserted, and have right-clicked to reveal the menu, just left click on the Paste option that is highlighted on the menu, and the text will be inserted as follows:

Insert copied text after this colon: **text that I want to highlight and copy.**

So, the bolded text to the right, in the sentence above, was Pasted into the selected position from the Virtual Clipboard.

How To Cut and Paste

As with Copy and Paste, I have found that many beginners have trouble with this concept at first. If you don't understand how this works you will not be able to fully benefit from the experience of sending/receiving e-mails and surfing the Net.

The ability to Cut and Paste is especially useful when you are replying to e-mails or when you find some text or graphics on a webpage that you would like to paste into one of your own documents.

You Cut and Paste whenever you want to remove some text or graphics from one place and insert it into another place.

A Cut and Paste operation is almost identical to Copy and Paste with the important exception that the Cut part of the operation is destructive. This means that once you have highlighted and Cut a portion of text, the Cut text is removed from the original location and placed into the virtual Clipboard for pasting elsewhere.

Otherwise, in order to Cut and Paste you follow the same steps that are shown above for Copy and Paste, as follows:

1. Before cutting the text you want to move, you first have to highlight it. To do this, place the cursor at one end of the text that you want to move.

2. Second, you left lick on your mouse button and HOLD the button down.

3. With the mouse button STILL depressed, drag the mouse across the text you want to remove. You will see that it gets highlighted with a black background.

4. When you reach the end point of the text that you want to cut, release the mouse button that you have been holding down. You will see that the text remains highlighted in black. This tells the program that you are working with that you want to perform an operation on that text that you just highlighted.

Here's a sample sentence with text that I want to highlight and cut.

5. Now that the text is highlighted, you can cut it by right-clicking on a portion of the highlighted text and choosing the Cut function from the menu that appears, as follows:

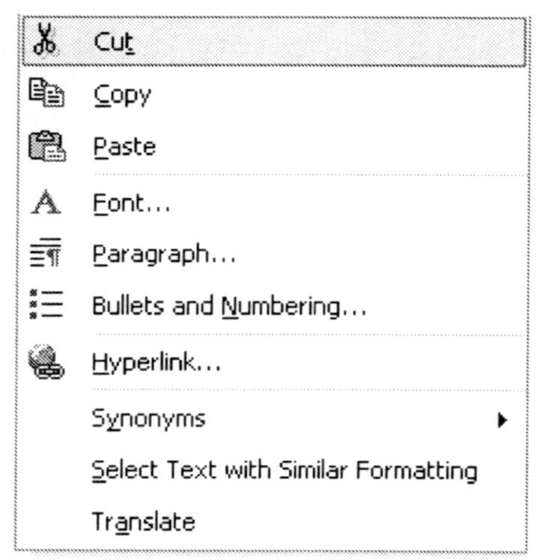

6. Left-click on the Cut item that is highlighted on the menu. That will save a copy of the text that you have just cut to the virtual Clipboard from which you can later access it and use it whenever you like.

7. Now that you have Cut the text, you will want to Paste it wherever else you want it to appear in your document. To do that, go to the exact place in your document where you want to insert the copied text. For example, to Paste the text you just cut out above, just below this paragraph, you simply position your cursor at the point where you want the text to be inserted, as follows:

8. Then, right-click at that point to display the edit options menu as follows:

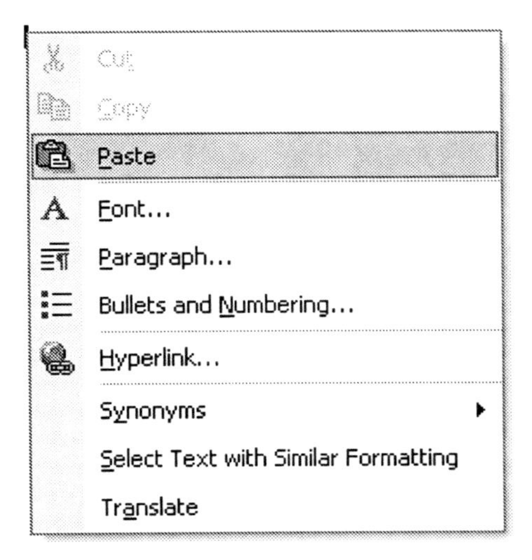

9. Once you have positioned the cursor in the exact position in your document where you want the text to be inserted, and have right-clicked to reveal the above menu, just left click on the Paste option that is highlighted there, and the text will be inserted as follows:

Insert cut text after this colon**: text that I want to highlight and cut.**

So, the bolded text to the right in the sentence above was Pasted into the selected position from the Virtual Clipboard.

HOW TO SEND, RECEIVE, MANAGE E-MAILS

Before getting into the mechanics of sending and receiving e-mails there are a few minor points that I need to discuss in order to reduce some of the general confusion that exists on the subject of sending and receiving e-mails.

E-Mail Overview

Even many people who already send and receive e-mails don't really understand the basics of what they are doing and how it works. This lack of basic understanding often leads to confusion and miscommunication.

How E-Mail Works

There are two main ways in which e-mail is sent, process and managed online; PC-based and Web-based.

PC-Based E-Mail

In this case, an e-mail software program runs on your local PC. So, all operations other than the actual transmission of the e-mail take place on your computer. The following diagram depicts the typical PC-based e-mail process:

E-Mail Process – PC-Based

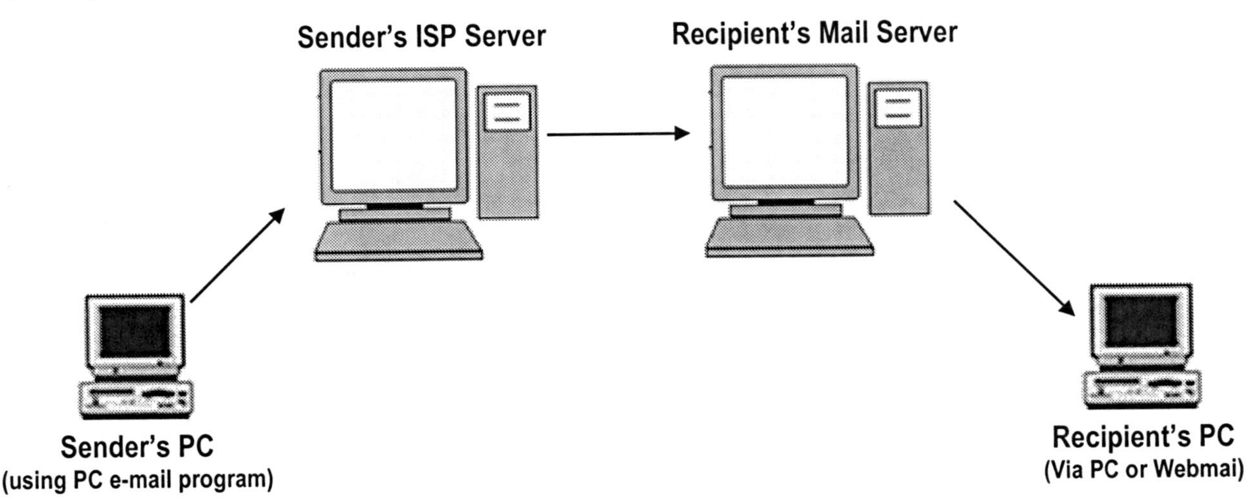

The main point to understand about PC-based e-mail is that you are NOT sending your e-mail directly to the personal computer of your addressee.

You are in fact sending it from your PC to the e-mail server of your ISP company. Your ISP then forwards your e-mail to the ISP or Webmail service of your intended recipient.

Whenever your intended recipient checks their e-mail via their PC-based e-mail program or their Web-based service, your e-mail is then downloaded from their ISP's server to their PC e-mail program or their browser (for Webmail) so they can read it.

Web-Based E-Mail

With a Web-based e-mail set-up, all operations related to sending/receiving your e-mails run on a program that is based on a remote website. Once you connect to that website via your browser, all operations take place there, rather than on your PC. For example, before you can send/receive e-mails via the hotmail service you must first use your browser to sign-in at hotmail. Here is a diagram of the Web-based e-mail process:

E-Mail Process – Web-Based

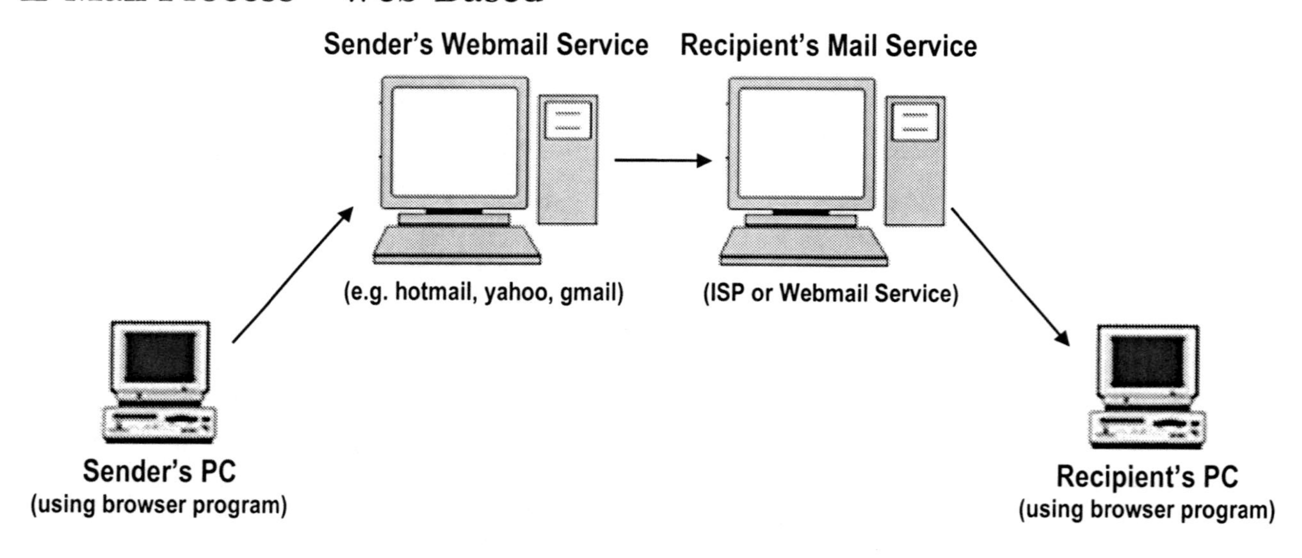

Just as with PC-based e-mail, using Web-based e-mail the e-mail message that you are sending does not go directly from your computer to the recipient.

First you must sign on via your account at the website of the Webmail Service you are using (e.g. hotmail.com). Then, all of your e-mail sending, receiving, and management is done online using the software of that Webmail service.

Once you click on Send, your Webmail service immediately transmits your e-mail to the recipient's Mail Service, which could be either a standard ISP, or a Webmail service such as google mail or hotmail.

For an example of Webmail services in action go to pages 73 and 81.

Note: Because neither one of the e-mail types discussed above goes directly from sender to receiver, there can never be certainty as to what will happen after you hit that Send button. And, you cannot count on the "Request Read Receipt" function that MS-Outlook and some other PC-based programs offer because the recipient can opt to NOT confirm receipt. Also, these functions don't work with Webmail services.

Pros and Cons of PC-Based E-Mail

Pros

Here are the Pros of using PC-based e-mail programs:

- PC-based e-mail is usually faster since you don't have to wait for info to be transferred back and forth through constant page refreshes every time you do something.

- Typical PC-based e-mail programs normally have more options and functions available for e-mail formatting, etc.

Cons

Here are the Cons of using PC-based e-mail programs:

- You normally have to pay for a PC-based e-mail program (e.g. MS-Outlook), either when you buy software for your computer or when you signup with an ISP.

- PC-based e-mail is more susceptible to viruses since it downloads the e-mails directly to your computer; meaning that aggressive anti-virus measures are necessary.

Pros and Cons of Web-Based E-Mail

Pros

Here are the Pros of using Web-based e-mail services:

- Services such as hotmail, gmail, yahoo mail and others are free, easy and convenient for the average non-business Internet user.
- Webmail-based services provide a level of insulation from Internet viruses since the e-mail and attachments are opened online and not on your PC.
- Your webmail account can be easily accessed from anywhere in the world as long as you have Internet access.

Cons

Here are the Cons of using Web-based e-mail services:

- Free Web-based e-mail services force the user to sign-on, send and receive e-mail in an environment where they are exposed to unwanted advertising and other unsolicited distractions.
- Web-based e-mail can be slow to work with since every time you make a change or update something it causes your browser to refresh.
- Most Web-based e-mail services do not have the full range of options that are available for composing and formatting e-mails that PC-based programs typically have.
- Free Web-based e-mail services are NOT used by serious businesses; so users of those services are never taken seriously by business users.

Bottom Line: If it's for personal use and you can live with the above Cons, by all means go with a free Webmail service. If it's for business purposes, stick with a PC-based e-mail program.

E-Mail Programs Used In This Guide

As covered earlier, for the purposes of this guide I have decided to use the Microsoft Outlook Express as the primary e-mail program for demonstration purposes in the real-life screen shots. I have chosen MS-Outlook because it is by far the most widely used PC-based e-mail program. As I write this it is estimated that more than 60% of all e-mailers use some version of MS-Outlook.

That figure is likely much higher when it comes to business users. Serious business users do not generally use Web-based e-mail services, and they definitely do not use free Webmail services like hotmail, google mail, or yahoo mail.

Nevertheless, I am also including two sections later on that show how to work with the most widely-used Web-based e-mail services: Hotmail and Yahoo! Mail. Based on the more than 30,000 people who have signed up for my various writing help courses, these two are definitely the most popular Web-based e-mail service used online, as I write this. Google Mail ranks third, right after these two.

In practical terms it really doesn't matter which e-mail program or service you use.

That's because most primary e-mail functions are generic in nature in any case, so all of the MS-Outlook, Hotmail and Yahoo! Mail functions that are shown in the examples throughout this guide will have very similar functionality in almost all other e-mail programs, whether they are PC-based or Web-based.

How To Set Up For E-Mail

Before you actually start sending e-mails and receiving e-mails there are a few things you need to know and do. First, you need to know some basic points about what your e-mail program toolbar looks like and what the basic functions are.

In addition, you also have to do a one-time set-up of your e-mail accounts in your e-mail program so that it will be able to communicate properly with the Internet in order to send and receive your e-mails. (i.e. MS-Outlook Express).

There are also some basic settings and options you will want to select before you start sending/receiving e-mails. These include choosing how your e-mail screen will be laid out, setting the text size for easy reading, and selecting other available options.

Typical E-Mail Program Toolbars

Below are the e-mail management toolbars for both MS-Outlook (PC-based) and MSN-Hotmail (Web-based). As you can see, although they are laid out differently, they both have very similar e-mail management functions.

MS-Outlook E-mail Toolbar

MSN Hotmail E-mail Toolbar

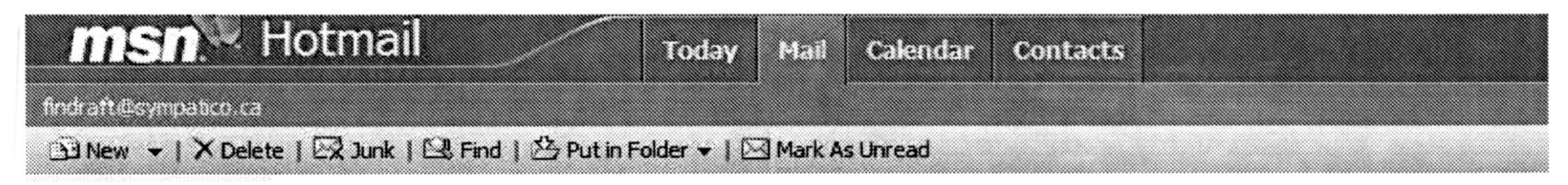

I've included the Hotmail toolbar here simply for comparison purposes. Essentially, regardless of which e-mail program you may be using, the basic functionality will be very similar. After all, the fundamental purpose of an e-mail program is to send and receive e-mails. Anything else is beyond that is all "bells and whistles".

Now, let's take a look at the MS-Outlook toolbar and see what each of the major functions does. For the purpose of this explanation I will refer to each function as either a function or a button. Most of these are covered in more detail later on.

This is the first button to click when you want to create new e-mail. When you click on this button it Opens a Create Mail Window in which you compose your e-mail.

Click on this button whenever you want to send an e-mail reply to the ONE originator of the e-mail that is currently highlighted in your Inbox. This Opens a Create Mail Window in which you compose your reply.

Click on this button whenever you want to send an e-mail reply to ALL recipients of the e-mail that is currently highlighted in your Inbox. This Opens a Create Mail Window in which you compose your reply.

The Forward button allows you to send copies of the e-mail that is currently highlighted in your Inbox to whomever you choose. This Opens a Create Mail Window in which you choose/add the recipients.

This button allows you to print a copy of the e-mail that is currently highlighted in your Inbox. Clicking on it will Opens the standard Windows Print Dialogue Box.

One click on this button will Delete the e-mail that is currently highlighted in whichever e-mail folder you are currently in. Be sure that you want to Delete the item before clicking on this button.

Clicking on this button will immediately send the e-mail that you have just composed and/or receive any e-mails from your ISP's server that are addressed to your e-mail account(s).

This button takes you to your Address Book where you can manage the e-mail addresses on your list (i.e. Add, Delete, Modify). This is normally an occasional maintenance function

This function allows you to find items in your e-mail folders or in specific e-mail messages. When you click on this button it Opens a dialogue box that lets you specify specific search values.

In addition to the above standard e-mail management buttons, MS-Outlook also includes a small 6-function toolbar just above them, to the left, as follows:

When you click on any one of the functions on this toolbar, a drop-down menu with multiple functions is displayed. For the purpose of this beginners guide I will not be covering the details of each dropdown menu item since most of the functions are just not required in day-to-day e-mailing.

Nevertheless, I will go over a few of the dropdown menu functions as they arise in the appropriate sections of this guide.

How To Set Up An E-Mail Account

This refers to setting up an e-mail account(s) in your e-mail program. This IS NOT about setting up an initial account with your ISP or your Web Mail Service. It is assumed that you are already signed up and ready to go with your ISP mail service.

The reason you need to set up accounts in your e-mail program is so that you can tell that program where to check for your incoming e-mail, and through which account(s) it should send outgoing e-mail. For most people this will be quite straightforward since they will typically have one e-mail account.

Nevertheless, most e-mail programs are set-up to handle multiple sending/receiving accounts if need be.

In MS-Outlook Express, here is what you do to set up a new e-mail account:

On the top toolbar click on **Tools** and then **Accounts**, as follows:

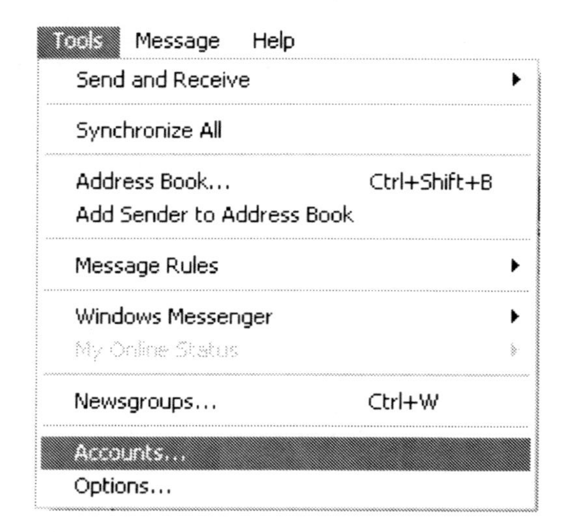

In the Internet Accounts Box, click on **Add** and then **Mail…** as shown below…

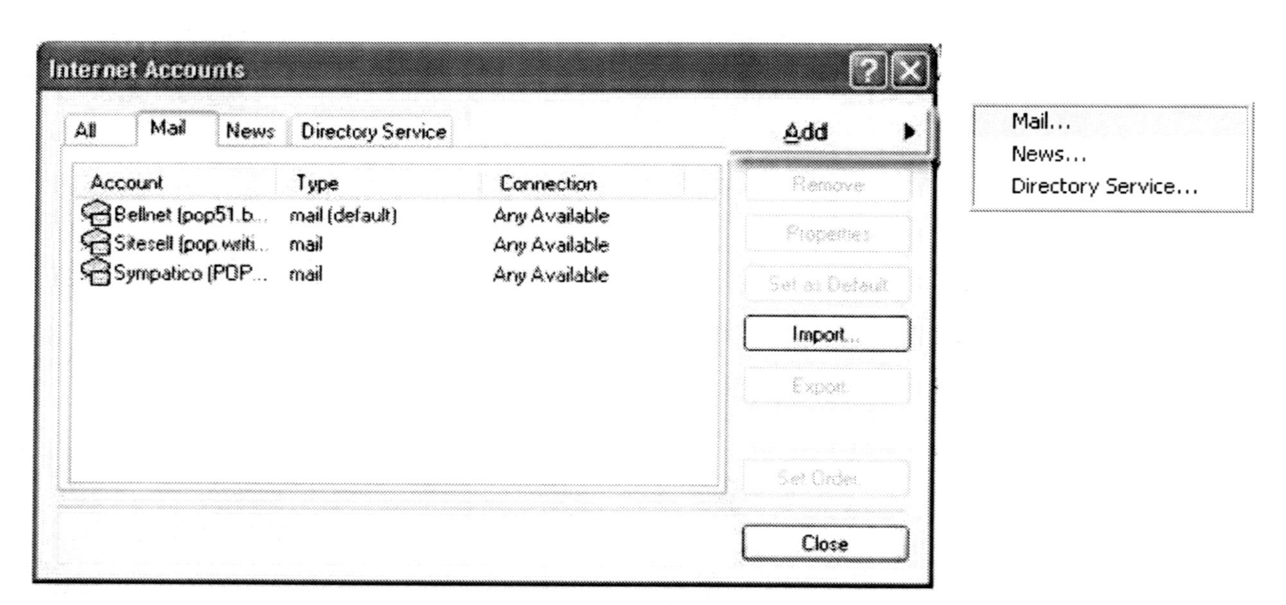

The accounts listed in the box above are my own business and personal accounts.

For the purposes of the following example, I am going to add a new account named "Demo Account" for illustration purposes. Once you click on **Mail…** a wizard will present you with a series of three Dialogue boxes asking for info regarding the specifics of the account, as follows…

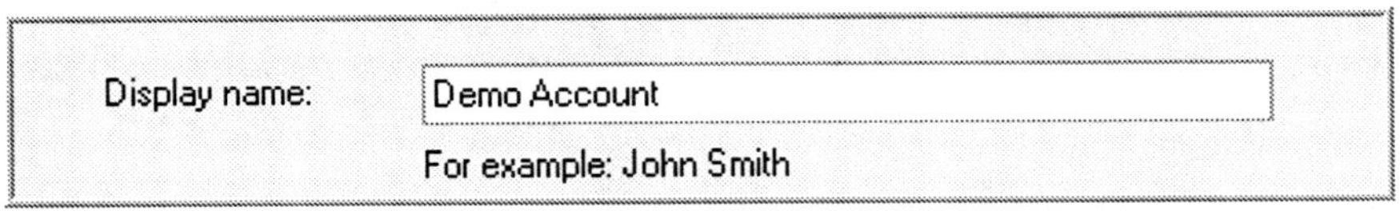

Display name: Demo Account
For example: John Smith

The Display Name you insert is the one that will appear in the "From" field of your outgoing e-mails. For this example I have chosen "Demo Account".

E-mail address: demoaccount@bellnet.ca
For example: someone@microsoft.com

Enter the E-Mail Address that you have set up at your ISP to which people will send you e-mails. For this example I used demoaccount@bellnet.ca.

Incoming mail (POP3, IMAP or HTTP) server:
pop51@bellnet.ca

An SMTP server is the server that is used for your outgoing e-mail.
Outgoing mail (SMTP) server:
smtp10.bellnet.ca

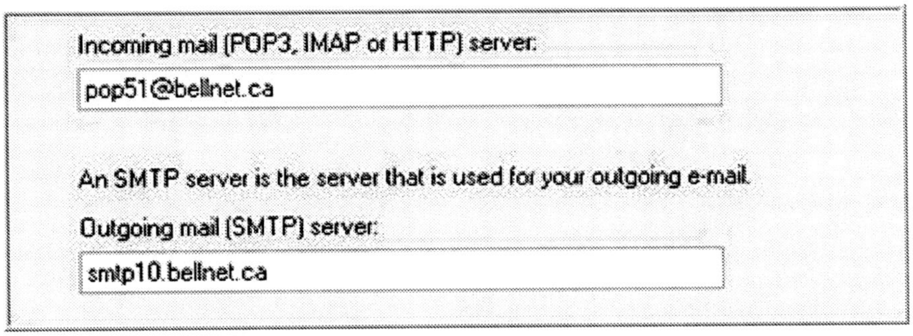

These two addresses are the most important entries in this process. The first address (i.e. pop51@bellnet.ca) tells the e-mail program exactly where to look on the Internet to retrieve Incoming e-mails addressed to you. The second field contains the address of the server (i.e. smtp10.bellnet.ca) that is set to process all of your Outgoing e-mails.

Both of these addresses will be supplied to you by your ISP when you set up your Internet access account. If you do not have them yet, contact your ISP to get them before trying to set up one of these accounts.

Once you have entered the above info just click on the "Finish" button to save it. Then, to review/verify your account settings, click on **Tools** and **Accounts** again. Notice that the new account that we just set up (i.e. "Demo") is now listed in the Internet Accounts box below.

To see the settings saved for an account, highlight it with your cursor and then click on the **Properties** button.

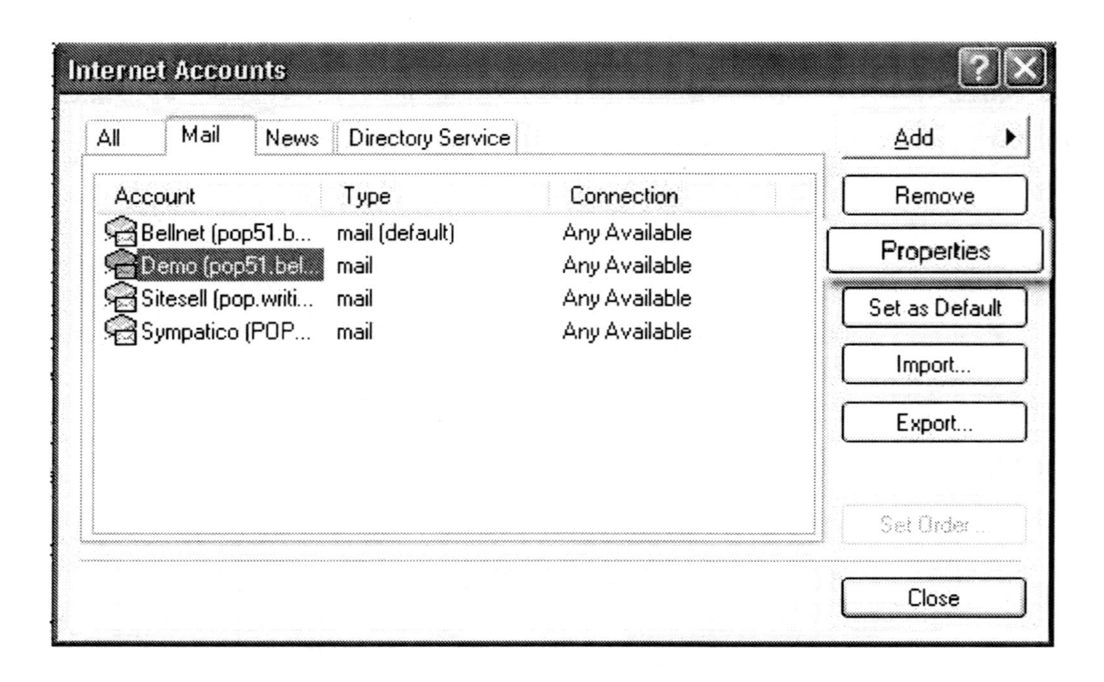

Clicking on the **General** and **Servers** tabs will show you all of the key settings for the account you have just set up. The other tabs are generally for more advanced users.

How To Set Up Your E-Mail Screen Layout

In MS-Outlook Express you have the option to change the layout of your e-mail viewing window. The layout that I use is the following:

- **Left-hand side:** list of all e-mail folders;
- **Upper-right side:** list of latest e-mails in current folder (i.e. Inbox in this case);
- **Lower-right side:** text of the current selected e-mail

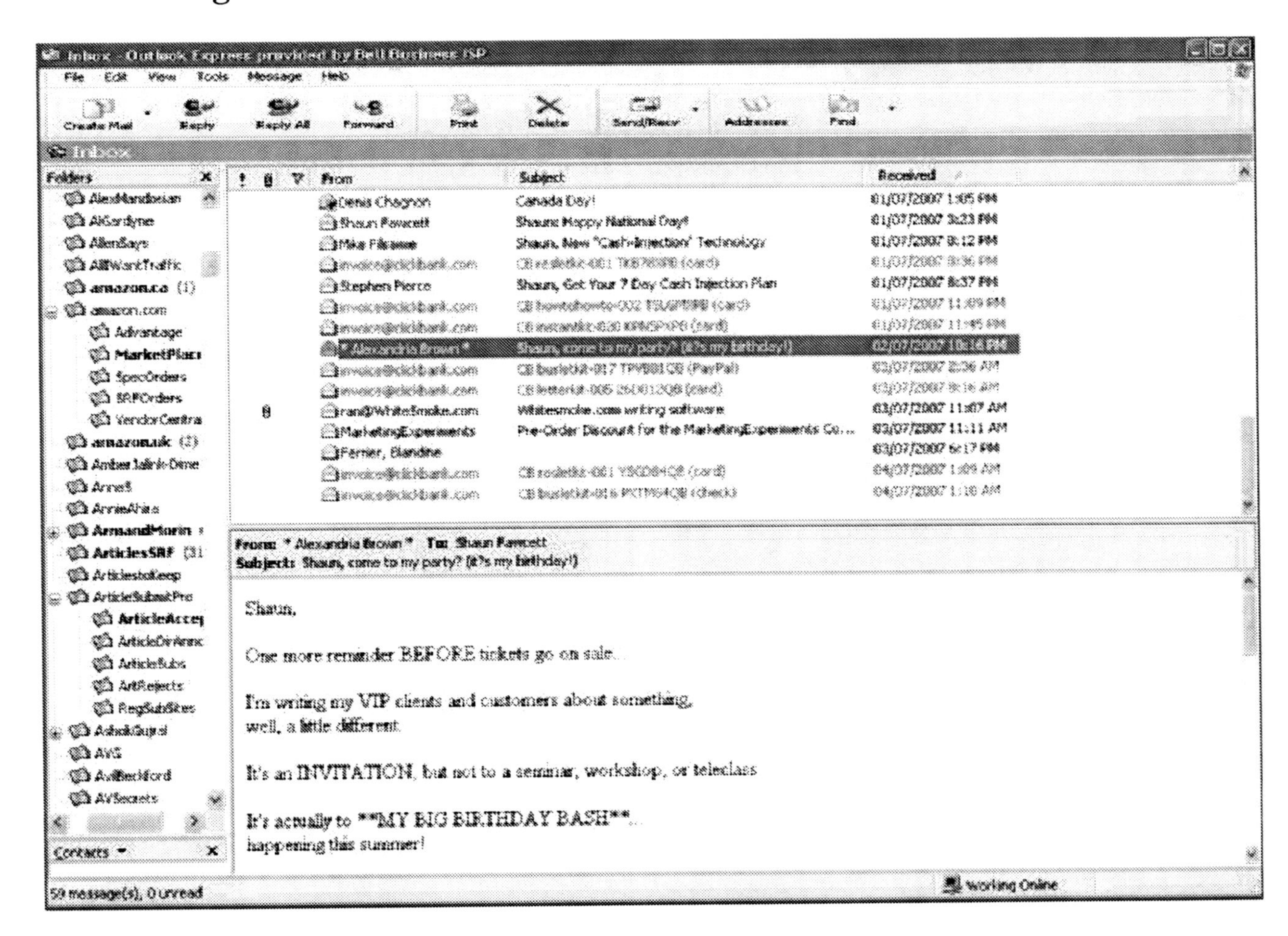

I prefer this layout because I can see everything at one time. You might like it too, because it gives you one-click access to whatever you want to look at next.

Nevertheless, there are other screen layout options as well. To check those out go to the dropdown toolbar in the upper left and click on **View** and then **Layout**. That will display a Window Layout Properties box like the following:

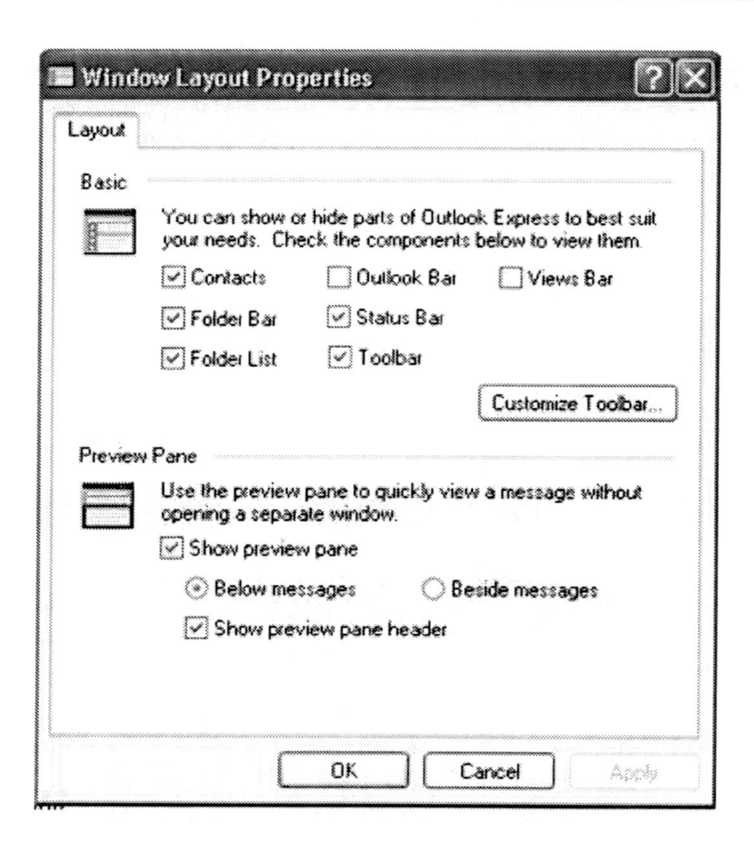

The checked boxes above correspond to the layout that I use, as per the screen layout shown on the previous page. As you can see, there are two Layout groupings; Basic and Preview Pane.

Take note that under Basic Properties there is a button that you can click on called "Customize Toolbar". This option will allow you to Add, Remove and/or Replace function buttons on your main e-mail functions toolbar. You might want to check out this option to see if it makes sense for you to customize your toolbar or whether you should stay with the default settings.

The only way you can decide what works best for you is to try the various options and see what they look like.

How To Change E-Mail Viewing Text Size

Many people find it difficult to read their e-mails on the screen at the default text size. This can be easily changed by clicking on **View** and then **Text Size** from the dropdown toolbar as follows.

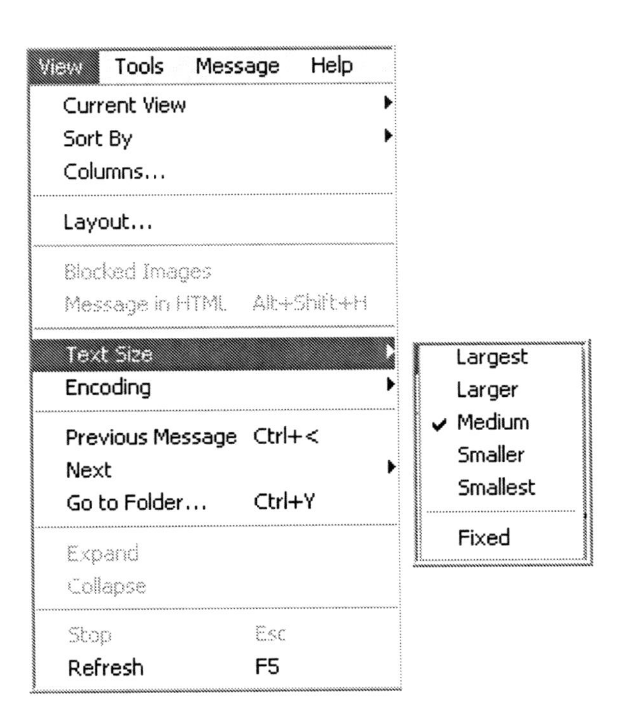

Just check your preference and it will be applied to the part of your e-mail viewing screen in which you view the actual e-mails.

Please note that this setting pertains to viewing the e-mails on your screen. It does not actually change the point size of the actual e-mail. To see how to do that, refer to the information on page 38.

How To Set-Up or Adjust E-Mail Options

On the top toolbar click on **Tools** and then **Options**, as follows:

E-Mail Options Settings Tabs

The E-mail Options Window in MS- Outlook Express is where you can set up ALL of your preferences related to the sending and receiving of your e-mails.

Since this guide deals strictly with the basics, I am only going to cover five (5) of the Options Tabs: **General, Read**, **Send**, **Compose** and **Spelling.** Feel free to explore the other tabs as you wish, but for the basics of sending/receiving e-mails, these five are the most important ones.

There is a very important point to remember whenever you change or adjust the settings in ANY one of the Tabs:

First; after you have made your changes, click on the **Apply** button on the bottom right of the Tab.

Second; click on **OK** on the bottom left to save the new settings and close the Tab..

Please Note: All of the settings applied in the Tabs that follow are as I have set them for my specific situation. You can change these to suit your own needs.

General Options Tab

The **General** Options tab is where you set-up your overall e-mail preferences; these settings are pretty well self-explanatory.

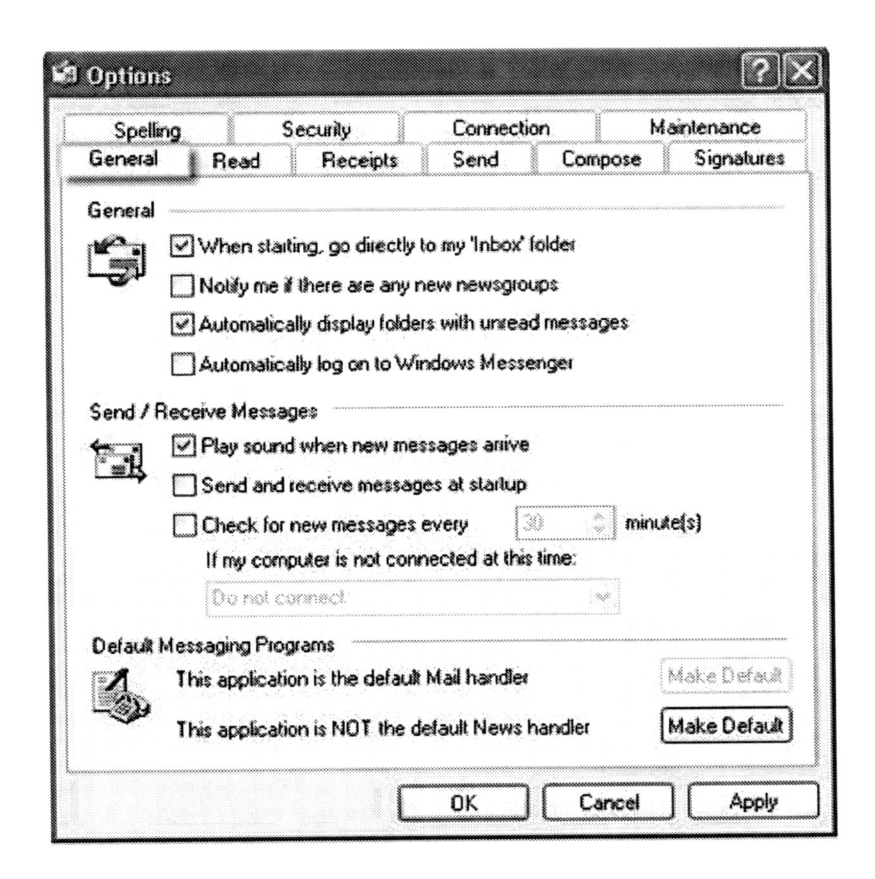

The reason why I Do Not send and receive e-mails at start-up or have them downloaded automatically every X minutes, is because I use another software tool to manually scan and view my e-mails before I read them into my e-mail program's Inbox. (See page 64).

Unless you are an advanced user I suggest you ignore ALL settings related to "news" or "Newsgroups".

Read Options Tab

The **Read** Options tab allows you to set your preferences as to when and how you want to read your incoming e-mails. The settings below are the ones that I use. You can adjust them to suit your own preferences.

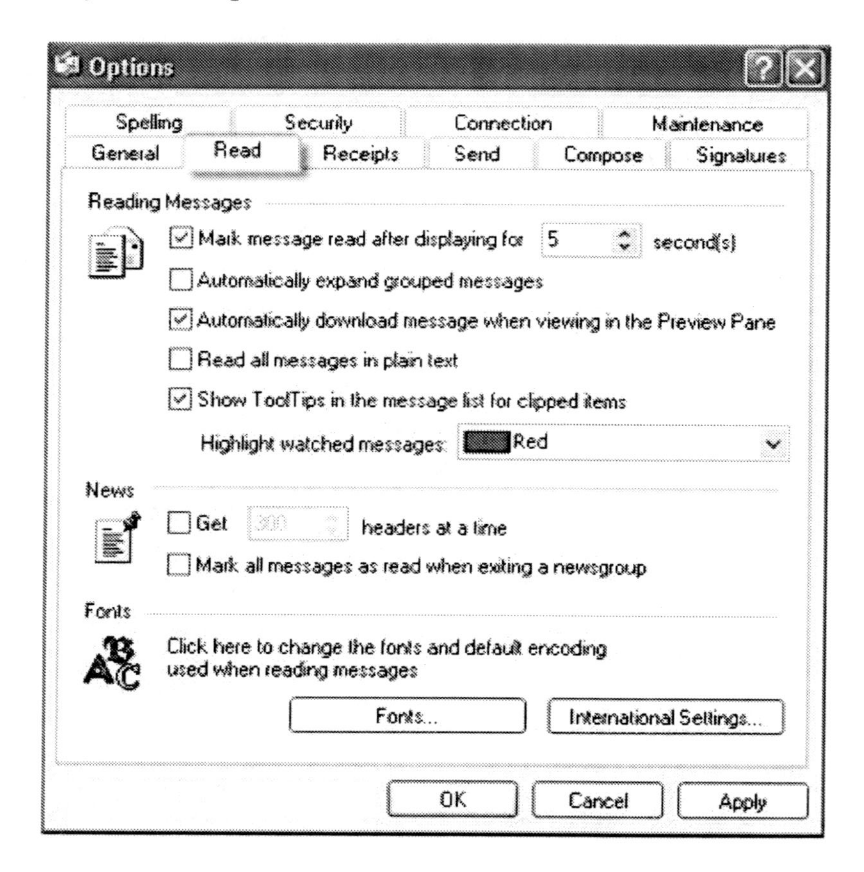

For reading standard e-mails, the five options listed under the "Reading Messages" heading are the important ones.

As I mentioned above, unless you are an advanced user ignore the "News" settings.

At the bottom of the tab you may change the "Fonts" for when your incoming e-mails display in the Inbox. I have never really understood the need for changing this, so I just leave it and stick with the default settings.

However, if you receive a lot of e-mails that use a character set other than Western/European it may be helpful to adjust how those e-mails will display.

Send Options Tab

The **Send** Options tab allows you to manage exactly how and when you want to send your e-mails and how you want them handled by the e-mail program.

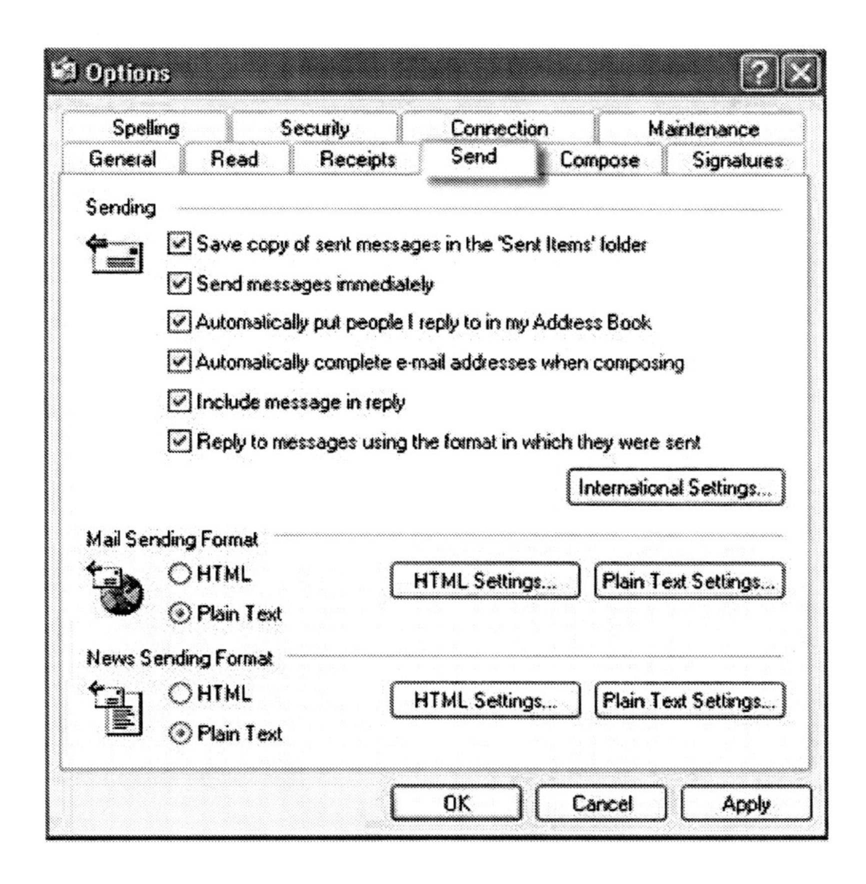

The “Sending” settings above are mostly self-explanatory, so I’m not going to explain the obvious, one-by-one.

Unless you are an advanced user who understands HTML formatting, keep the “Mail Sending Format” set to “Plain Text”.

Again, unless you are an advanced user ignore the “News” settings.

Compose Options Tab

The **Compose** Options tab allows you to control the look of your outgoing e-mails.

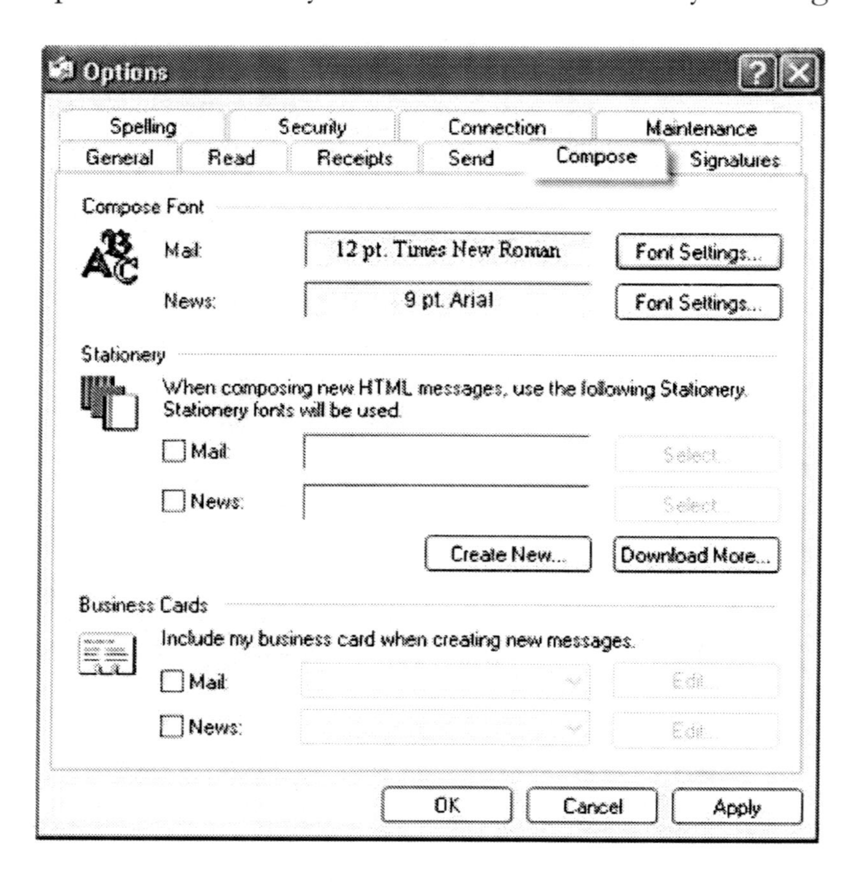

The "Compose Font" option above is the most important. Make sure you use a readable font style with a size within normal reading limits. I can't tell you how many times I have received e-mails from people with teensy, weensy characters that I had to increase in size just to be able to read them. Even worse, are receiving e-mails with giant letters caused by the point size being set to 16 or 20, or larger.

I recommend you use a standard business size of 12 point Times New Roman. If your audience has vision problems you could increase that to 14 pt. but don't exceed that.

The "Stationery" option allows you to set a standard background color, pattern or design for all of your outgoing e-mails. I cover that later on page 47.

Spelling Options Tab

The **Spelling** Options tab allows you to specify whether you want your outgoing e-mails spell-checked and, if so, exactly how you want it to be done.

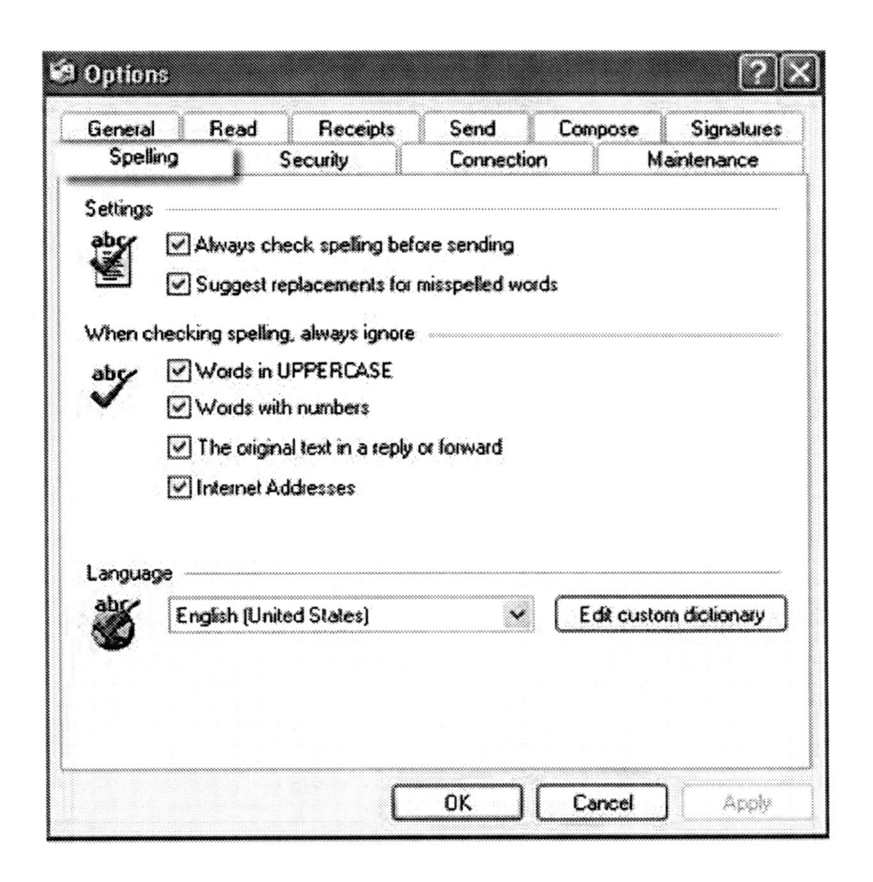

As you can see by the fact that all of the above boxes are checked I use full spell-checking before my e-mails are sent.

Based on the vast majority of e-mails I receive every day, I highly recommend that you select these spell-checking options too! I am always surprised by how many typos I make composing my e-mails. Fortunately my spell-checker catches most of them so I can fix them before an e-mail goes out. I think there is a tendency to make errors when composing e-mails since they are often typed in a hurry.

Sending out e-mails riddled with typos is unprofessional in business and disrespectful for social correspondence. It's worth the extra minute it takes to get the spelling right.

How To Compose and Send E-Mails

Once you are familiar with all of the basic concepts covered in the previous sections, the actual composing and sending of a simple e-mail will be easy.

In addition to composing and sending a basic e-mail there are a couple of related things you will want to do from time to time. These are: sending/forwarding copies to third parties, and sending your e-mail with documents attached.

How To Compose An E-Mail

First, you click on the Create Mail button on the e-mail toolbar, as follows:

Clicking on the Create e-mail button will open a compose e-mail window like this:

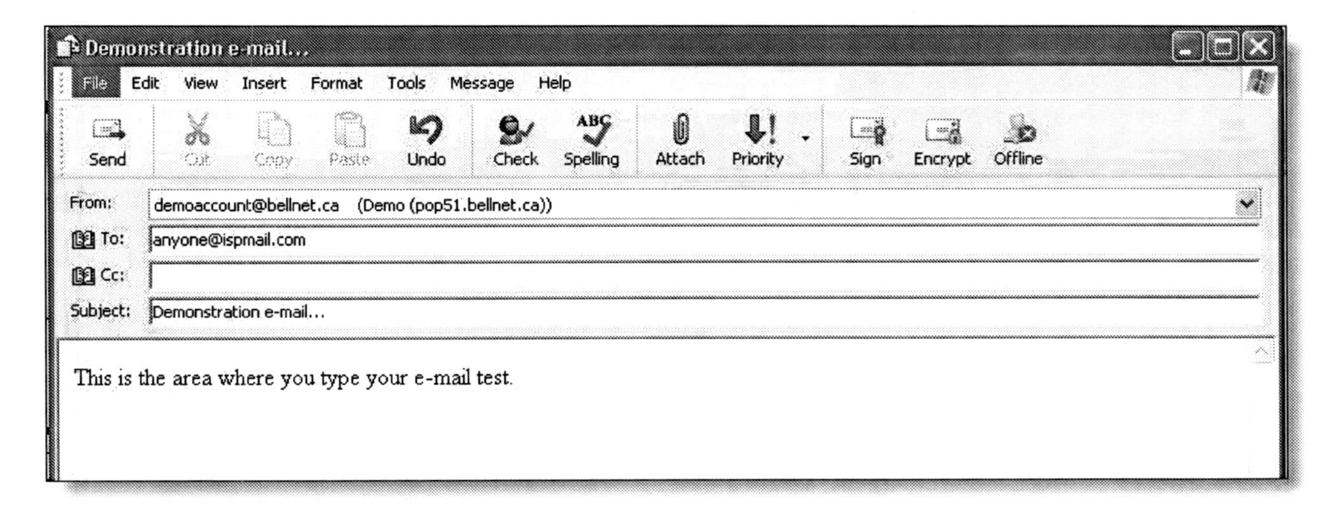

Enter the e-mail address of the intended recipient in the "To:" field. Then enter a short subject that describes the content of your e-mail in the "Subject:" field.

After that you can type in the text of your e-mail in the e-mail text box as shown in the figure above. That's it. You have composed an e-mail and are ready to send it.

How To Send an E-Mail

Once you have composed your e-mail as shown in the previous step, to send the e-mail you simply click on the Send Button on the left end of the e-mail toolbar.

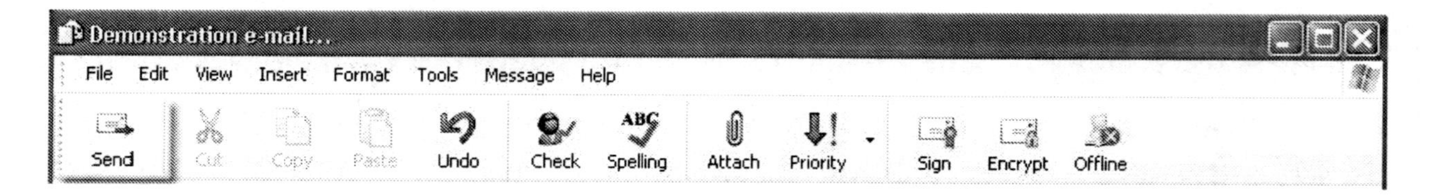

Notice how what was the "Create Mail" button on the e-mail toolbar in Compose mode has been transformed into the "Send" button when the toolbar is displayed in the Send mode.

How To Spell-Check Outgoing E-Mails

If you have the spell-checking function enabled (see page 41) a spell-checker box will pop up at this point if it has detected any problems with the text of your e-mail.

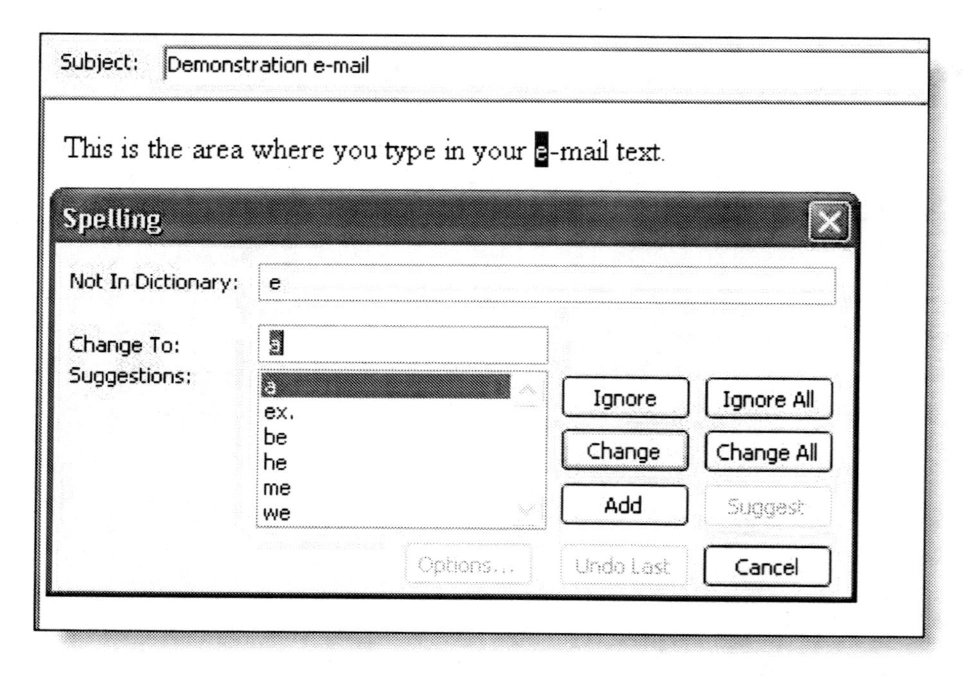

In this case the spell-checker is objecting to the "e" in e-mail which it highlights because that particular term is not listed in its internal dictionary. Since I am ok with that I simply click on the "Ignore" button. If you want to use one of the suggestions in the list, highlight it and click on the "Change" button and it will insert the new term.

How To Use the Address Book

MS Outlook Express automatically stores the names and e-mail addresses of all e-mails that you Send and Receive into your Address Book unless you tell it not to. I recommend that you leave the default setting and allow this to happen.

To use the Address Book when sending an e-mail just click on the little address book icon to the left of "To:". This will open the "Select Recipients" window as per below.

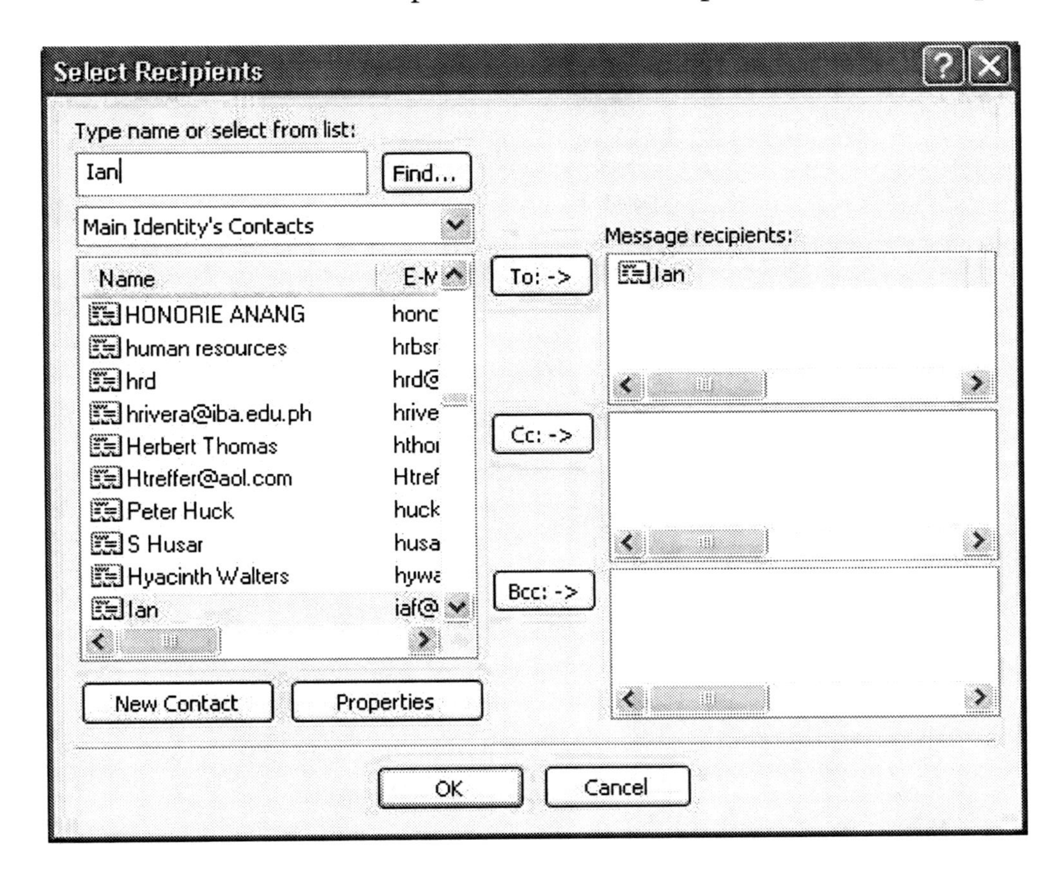

In this case I typed "Ian" my brother's name into the "Find…" box on the upper left and it immediately highlighted Ian's name and e-mail address in the Search Results Box on the lower left.

To Send the current e-mail to Ian, I simply click on the "To:->" button on the upper right and the program inserts the currently highlighted name and e-mail address into the "To:" field of the current e-mail. Click on the OK Button to complete the operation and close the "Select Recipients" window.

How To Send Copies To Others

To send copies of your e-mail to "other people" in addition to the primary recipient that you have specified in the "To:" field; enter each e-mail address into the field marked "Cc:" as per below. Be sure to separate the e-mail addresses with semi-colons.

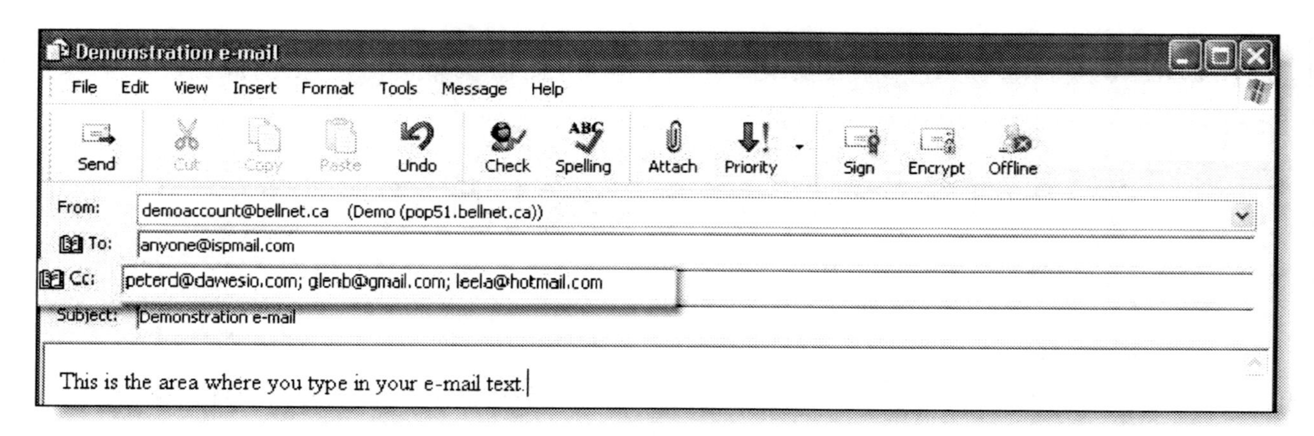

By the way, the term "Cc:" stands for Carbon Copy (ies). It is a term that has been carried over in business circles from the days before photocopiers, when extra copies of documents were created by placing a piece of carbon paper under the original in order to transfer a copy to a blank sheet of paper underneath.

It is possible to add multiple addresses into the "To:" field as well, if you like. But the standard way to send a copy of your e-mail to multiple recipients is via the "Cc:" field.

Be very careful when choosing to send copies to everyone on your list via the Cc: function. Everyone who is on the list will receive the complete list of names and e-mail addresses which in some cases will be an inappropriate breach of privacy.

If you want to send copies to everyone but not compromise everyone's privacy make sure you use the "Bcc:" function which is available in the "Select Recipients" window shown on the previous page. Bcc: will cause copies to be sent to each address on the list BUT the list of all recipients/addressees will NOT be displayed in each e-mail.

So, if you are e-mailing to a group of friends that all know each other, "Cc:" is fine. Otherwise "Bcc:" is probably the most prudent choice.

How To Select Background Wallpaper

To choose a pattern or design rather than blank white as the background for your e-mails, click on the dropdown arrow to the right side of the Create Mail Button.

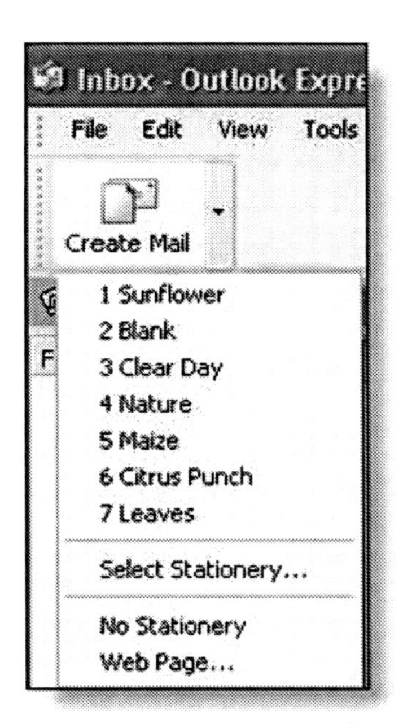

You can preview the look of each background before choosing one; each time you click on one of the options on the dropdown menu a "Compose Message" window will open with the pattern you have chosen displayed in the background.

If you don't like the pattern shown just close the Compose Message window and select another pattern from the dropdown list. As well, clicking on the "Select Stationery…" option will display additional choices that are not listed on the dropdown menu.

Once you have found a background pattern/color you like, just leave that window open and compose and send your e-mail.

A note of caution here; business users almost never use special backgrounds/patterns in their e-mails. It is almost always "newbies" who use these. So if you want to be taken seriously as a business and/or professional person, DO NOT use these.

How To Send An Attachment

To send a document such as a photo as an attachment to your e-mail; first click "Insert" on the toolbar at the top of the Compose Message window and then click on "File Attachment" on the dropdown menu.

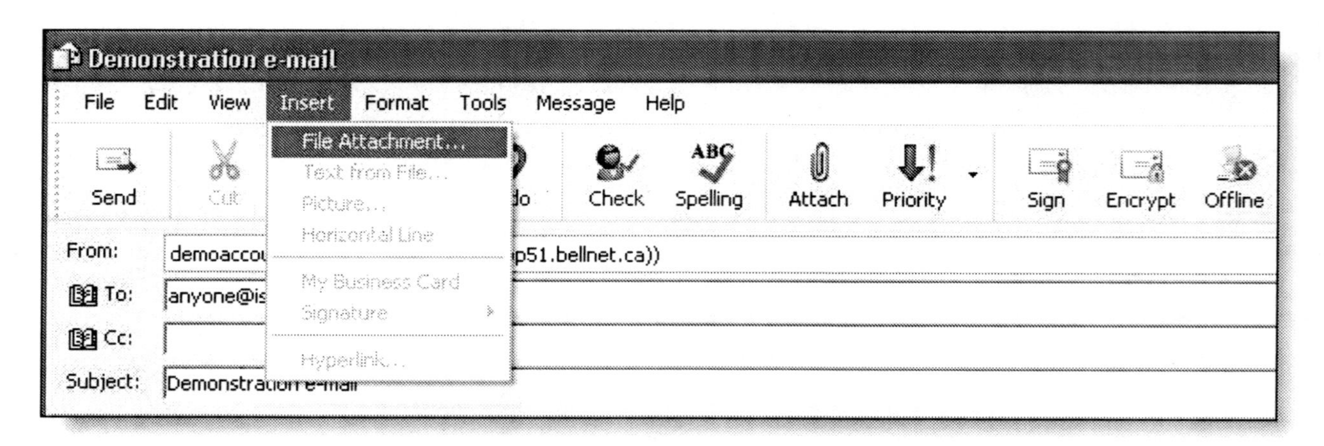

Clicking on the File Attachment menu item will open the Insert Attachment window:

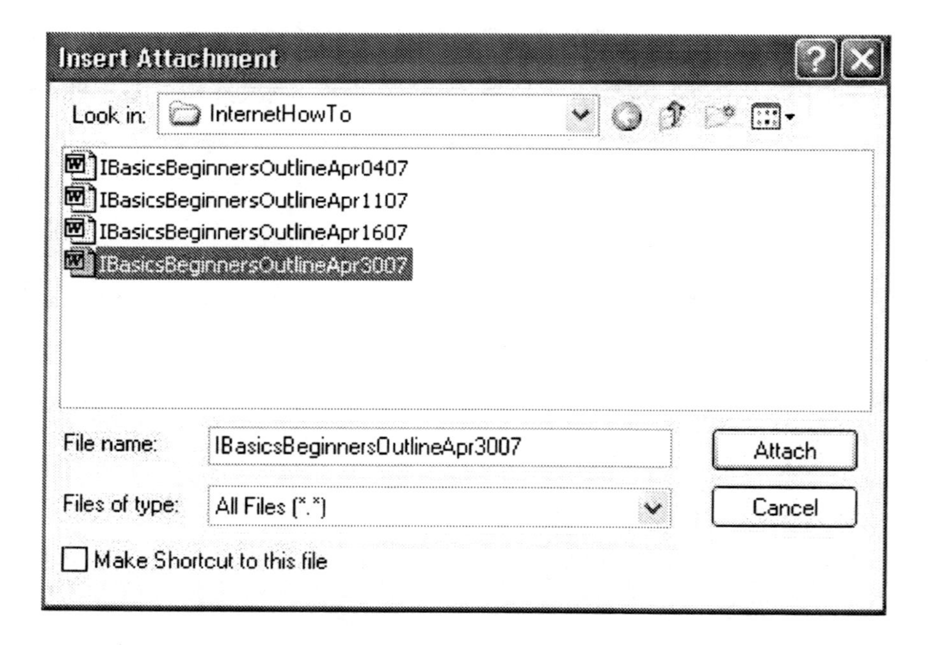

At this point you simply navigate through your folders to whatever file that you want to attach. Once you have highlighted that particular file, click on the "Attach" button and that window will close and reveal the Compose Message window again.

In the Compose Message window, the file name you selected will now be displayed next to the word "Attach:", immediately under the "Subject:" line.

How To Reply To E-Mails

There are a number of different ways that you can Reply to an e-mail.

First there is the straightforward simple reply back to the sender. Second, you may want to reply to the sender, plus everyone else on the sender's list. Finally, you may receive an e-mail that you simply want to pass-on or Forward to someone else.

How To Send A Simple Reply

A simple reply normally involves one sender and one receiver. You simply want to reply directly back to the person who sent you a particular e-mail.

First highlight the e-mail that you want to reply to in whatever folder you are in. (Normally, your Inbox).Then click the Reply button on the e-Mail Functions Toolbar.

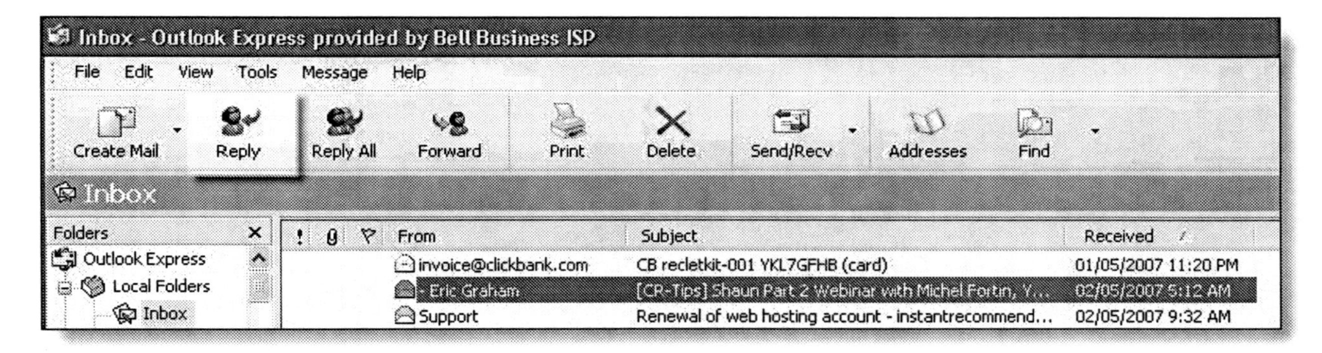

In the example above the e-mail being replied to is in the Inbox folder. However, you can reply to an e-mail from any folder. Just choose that folder, highlight the e-mail you want to reply to, and then hit the Reply button.

When you click on the Reply button a Compose E-mail Window will open so you can address the e-mail and add your text. As shown below, in Reply mode the e-mail program automatically inserts the text of the original e-mail into the bottom of your reply so that you have a trail or "thread" of what was sent previously.

This gives you easy reference access to exactly what was said before, and it allows you to quickly copy and paste snippets of the original e-mail into your part of the Reply.

Standard Compose E-Mail Window

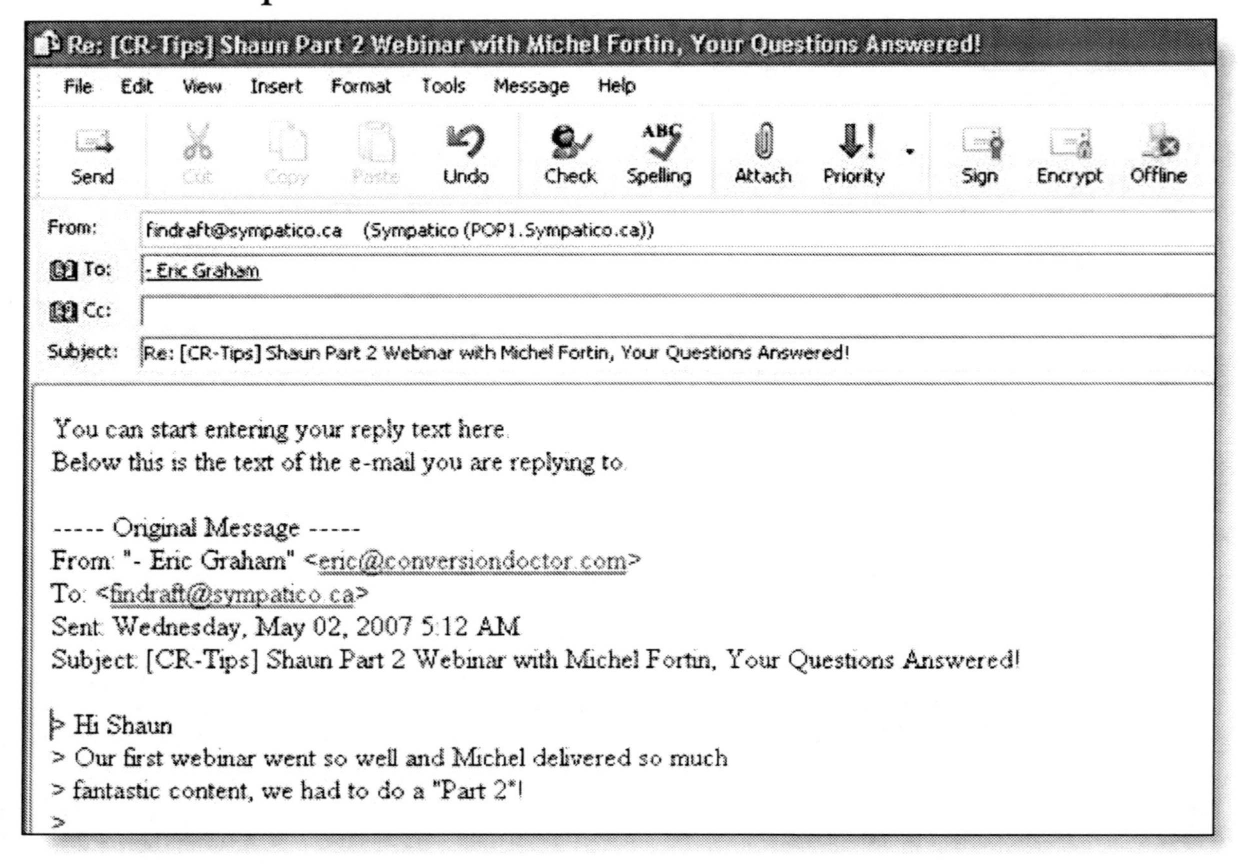

For a simple Reply, your e-mail program will automatically insert the e-mail address of the original sender into the "To:" field.

Also, the program will automatically insert "Re:" (stands for "Reply" or "Regarding") into the beginning of the "Subject:" field; thus making it clear to the eventual recipient that yours is a "Reply" to their e-mail.

Nevertheless, even with these helpful automatic insertions there can be a lot of confusion created once an e-mail exchange goes beyond the original single e-mail *out* with a single reply *back*.

For more information on this and how to properly and appropriately reply to an e-mail see the section on *About Replying To E-Mails* on page 53.

How To "Reply All"

You "Reply All" to an e-mail when the e-mail to which you are replying has multiple recipients and you want ALL of those recipients to also see your reply back to the original sender. Using the "Reply All" function will send your reply to ALL parties involved in the original e-mail; the sender, plus all others who received copies.

For example, say a friend or colleague sends an e-mail to you as well as to a number of other colleagues by using the "Cc:" function. You, clicking on the "Reply All" button will ensure that your reply to that e-mail goes to the original sender as well as to ALL other people who received that sender's original e-mail.

To do this, first highlight the e-mail that you want to reply to, and then click on the "Reply All" button on the E-Mail Functions Toolbar.

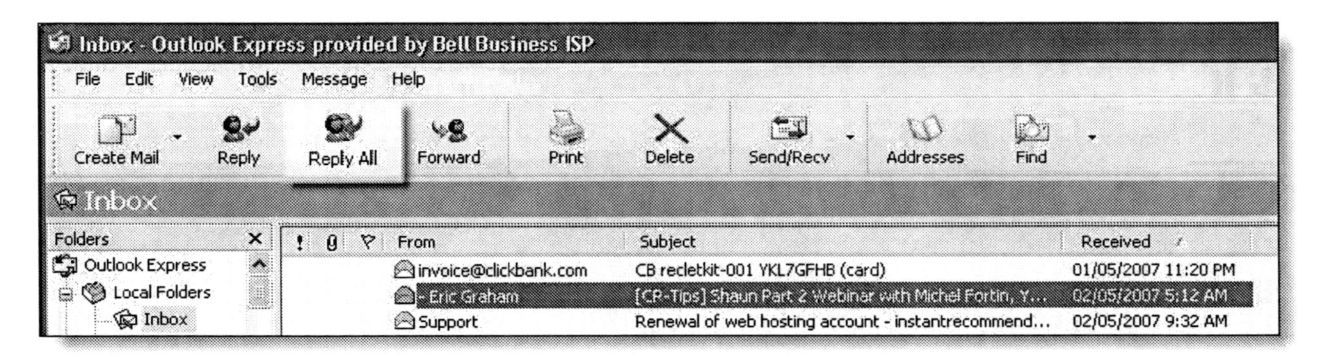

That will open the standard Compose E-Mail Window into your browser so that you may add your comments and then send your reply e-mail in the normal way; by hitting the Send button. (see Compose E-Mail Window on previous page).

In exactly the same way as when you do a simple e-mail Reply, when the Compose E-mail Window opens, the "To:" field addresses and "Subject:" will already be filled in. The text of the e-mail to which you are replying will also be included in the message field so that you can refer to it when you are adding your comments at the top of that box. (See *How To Send A Simple Reply*, on page 49 for details).

Think carefully before you "Reply All". Make sure it makes sense to reply back to ALL of those people. A single reply to the original sender might make more sense.

How To Forward An E-Mail

You Forward an e-mail when you want to pass along an exact copy of an e-mail that you received from someone else.

Typically, you will use the Forward function if you receive an e-mail and you want to pass it on because you believe that it may be if interest to a friend or colleague.

To Forward an e-mail, highlight the e-mail you want to pass on and then click on the Forward button on the e-Mail Functions Toolbar.

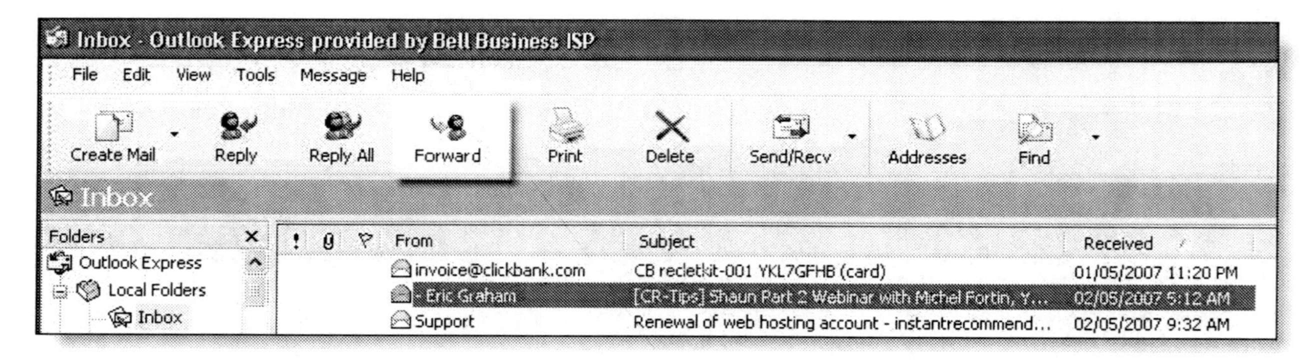

That will open the standard Compose E-Mail Window into your browser so that you may add your comments and then forward your e-mail in the normal way; by hitting the Send button. (See Compose E-Mail Window in the previous section).

In exactly the same way as when you do a simple e-mail Reply, when the Compose E-mail Window opens, the "To:" field addresses and "Subject:" will have already been filled in automatically by the program. Of course, the text of the message which you are forwarding will be in the message field. You can insert your own comments/remarks at the top of that box as you wish. (See *How To Send A Simple Reply*, page 49 for details).

SPAM WARNING:

Be careful when forwarding e-mails to others. Before you do, make sure that you believe it is absolutely necessary that you pass along the e-mail. Technically, Forwarding unsolicited e-mail indiscriminately to all and sundry makes you a spammer. **So, only Forward e-mails to others on an absolute "need to have" basis.**

About Replying To E-Mails

Replying to e-mails is one of the areas where the vast majority of e-mailers fall short. In this category, I am including the majority of experienced e-mailers too! It is not only beginners who are guilty of poor e-mail reply etiquette.

Here Is The General Rule:

To facilitate better communication via e-mail I STRONGLY SUGGEST that you Revise the Subject Line whenever replying to an e-mail so as to give it a meaningful title. Or, you will end up with a series of identically titled e-mails.

Imagine that a friend or colleague sends you an e-mail titled "Next Sunday's Get Together" in which they simply advise you of the time and location of an event and ask you to indicate whether you plan to attend.

However, as is often the case; that initial invitation e-mail results in a flurry of e-mails back-and-forth dealing with various related subjects such as: they can't make it until 4:00 p.m., should they bring anything?,. would they be willing to pick up a friend of yours, what's the friend's address?, etc., etc.

Based on what I have seen, at the end of all of this back-and-forth your mail folder will look something like the following.

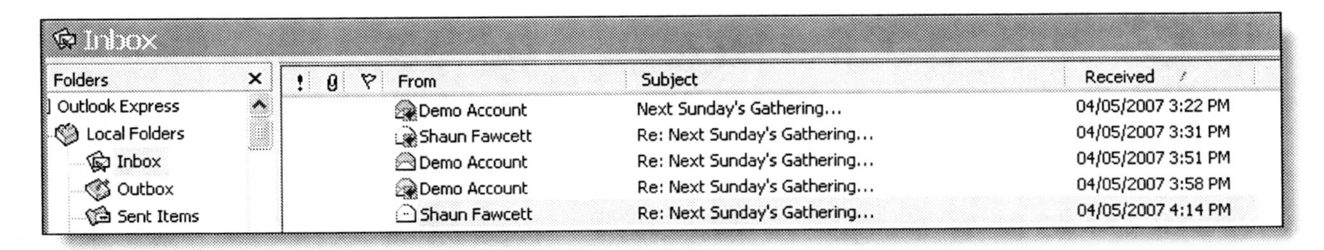

That is, your folder will end up with five (5) Subject lines that are exactly the same, as in: "Re: Next Sunday's Gathering". All you can tell by glancing at that mail folder (Inbox in this case) is that they all deal with the same overall subject. But two days later try to go back and figure out which one explains the revised arrival time, or which one says what to bring, or which contains the name and address of the friend, etc?

In reality it can be much worse than this example. In fact, I have often seen e-mail exchanges of 15 to 20 or more e-mails, each one with EXACTLY the same Subject title! This is ridiculous of course, but it happens all the time; even in business situations!

So, how does one deal with this? It's simple actually.

All you have to do to make the Subject Lines in your e-mail replies meaningful is add a relevant word or phrase at the leading end (i.e. left end) of the subject line.

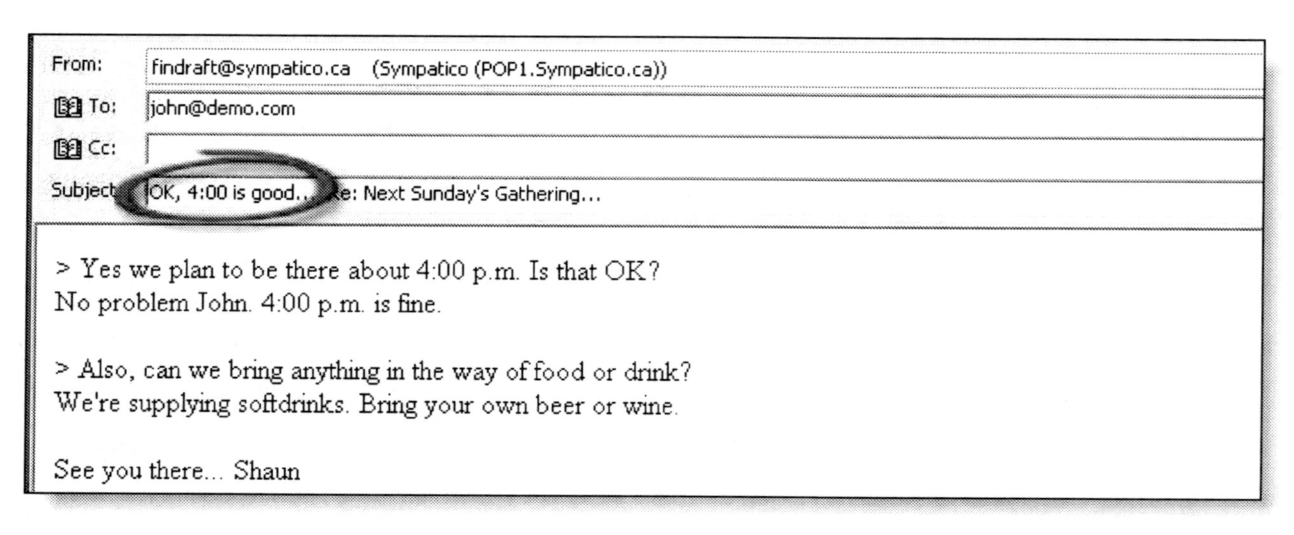

I think that a lot of people may be under the mistaken impression that they cannot change the Subject Line when they reply to an e-mail. This is NOT true of course. Just place your cursor anywhere in the reply Subject Line and make your revisions.

One other thing you can do to make your e-mail replies more meaningful is to copy and paste each specific point that you are addressing into your reply, one-by-one, and then respond to each point separately. The example above shows exactly how I do this when I reply to ALL e-mails that I receive.

This point-by-point reply approach is especially helpful when you receive e-mails that raise many different issues/questions. I receive lots of these. By addressing each point separately as shown in the above example, there will be no misunderstandings.

How To Manage Your E-Mails

Once you are familiar with all of the basic concepts covered in the previous sections, the actual composing, sending and replying to e-mails will be straightforward.

In addition to sending/receiving e-mails, there are a few other things that you need to know to effectively manage your e-mails once you have composed or received them.

Sending Your E-Mails

Once you have composed your e-mail, addressed it, and added any attachments if necessary, you will still need to actually Send it. To do that, you simply click on the Send Button on the toolbar at the top of the Compose E-Mail window.

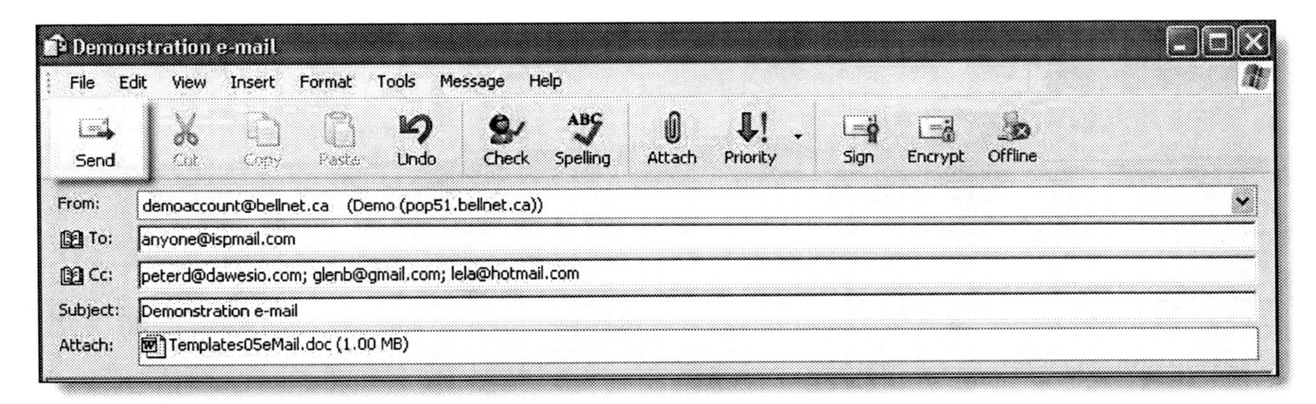

As soon as you click on the Send Button your e-mail program will instantly transmit your e-mail from your computer to the e-mail server used by the e-mail addressee. In reality, your e-mail will actually be uploaded from your computer to your ISP's e-mail server and then transmitted onward to the e-mail server of the recipient's ISP.

So, it is important to note here that the intended recipient of your e-mail will not actually receive it UNTIL they connect to their ISP's e-mail server and then actually check their e-mail account Inbox. (See page 21).

Therefore, E-mail is NOT instantaneous like a phone call because it will not be read until the addressee checks for it. So, you can never "assume" that your e-mail has been read just because it has been sent. If you want to be absolutely sure, you must check directly with the recipient.

Receiving Your E-Mails

To receive an e-mail you simply open your e-mail program and click on the Send/Receive Button on the main toolbar as shown below.

Once you click that button, and assuming that your computer is connected to the Internet, your e-mail program will download any e-mails addressed to you from your ISP's mail server and deposit those in your e-mail program's Inbox folder.

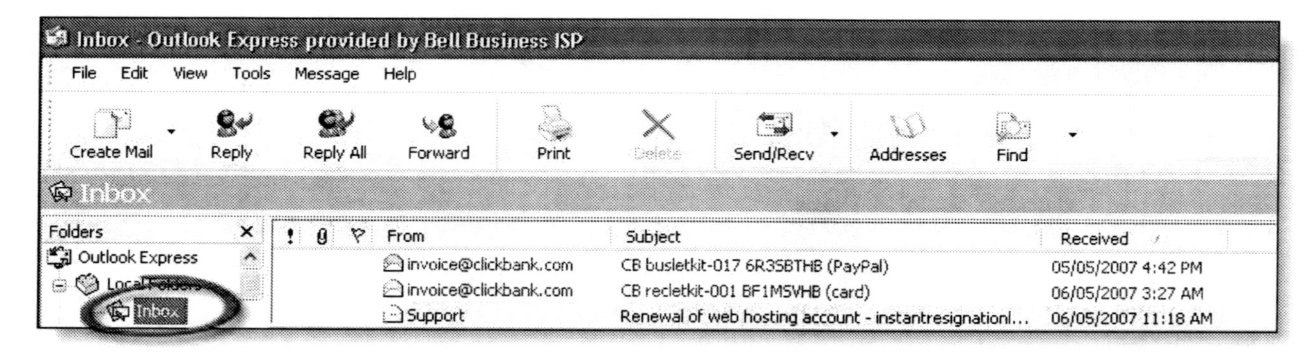

Once your new e-mails have been downloaded into your Inbox folder you can review them one-by-one in the reviewing pane and take action on each one, as appropriate.

How To Delete An E-Mail

To delete any e-mail (in any folder) highlight the e-mail in the review window and then click on the Delete Button on the main toolbar.

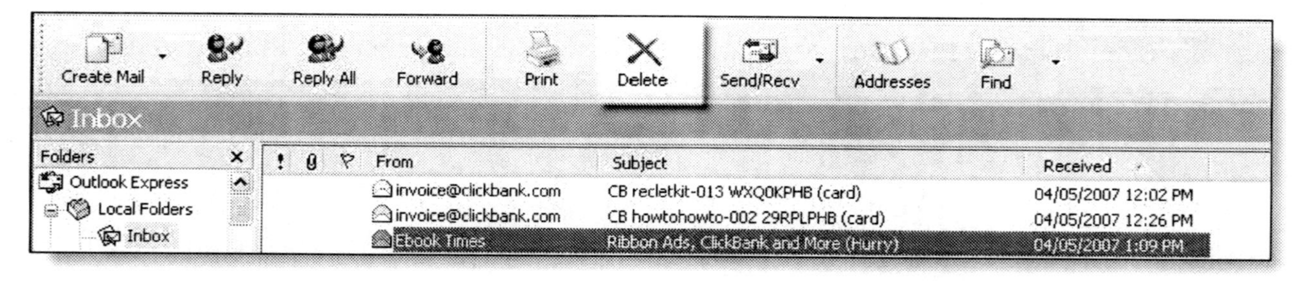

Or, as a shortcut, you can simply depress the Delete Key on your keyboard.

How To Print An E-Mail

Even though the advent of e-mail was supposed to reduce the use of paper, I find myself frequently printing out e-mails for one reason or another. I think that most people print them out from time-to-time. So here's how to do it.

To print out an e-mail, first click and highlight the e-mail that you want to print and then click on the Print Button on the E-mail Functions Toolbar as shown.

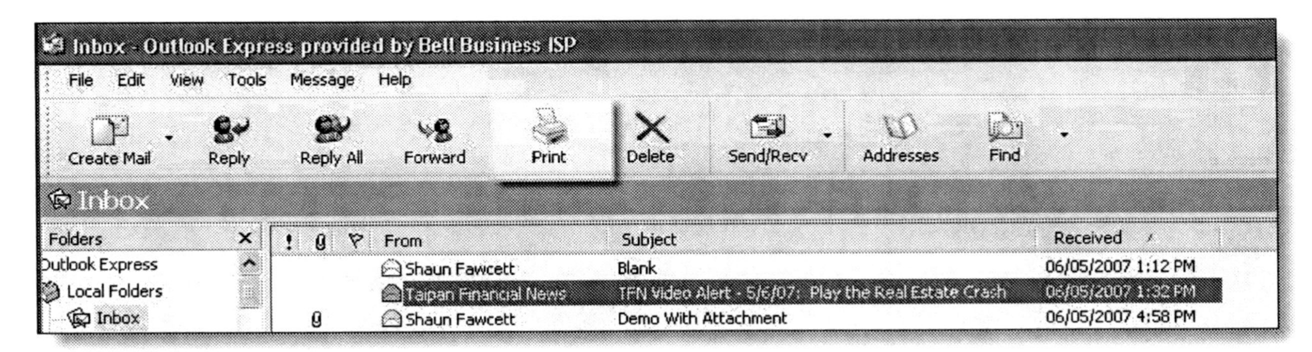

That will immediately open your computer operating system's standard Print Window:

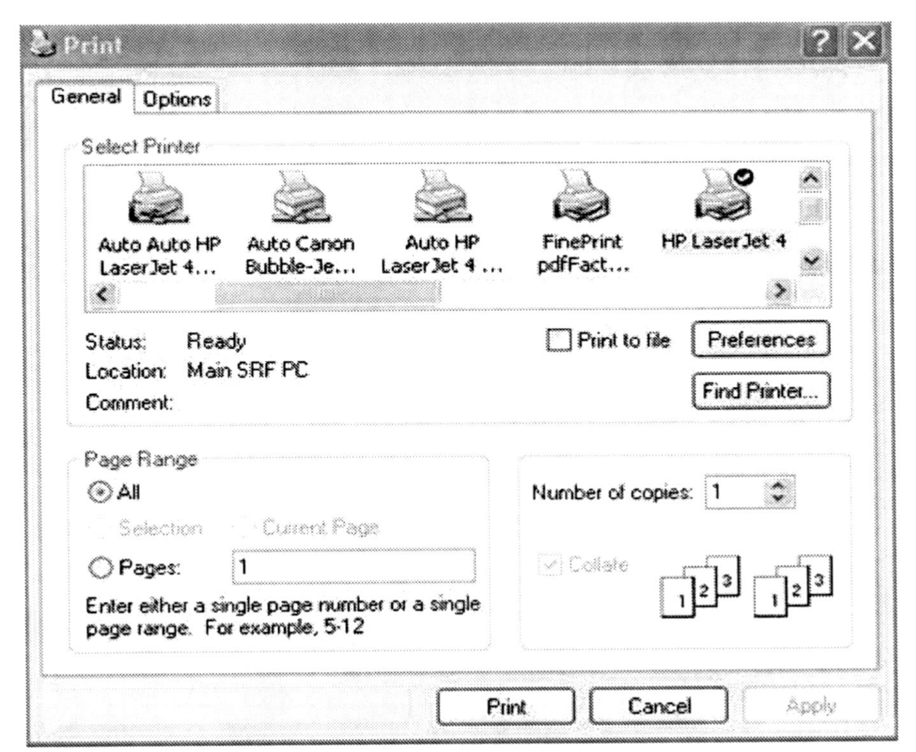

Adjust any Print Options if necessary; then click on the Print Button just as if you are printing from any other program.

How To Save An E-Mail

As you review each e-mail in your Inbox folder you will want to either Delete it or Save it. The normal way to Save e-mails is to move them from your Inbox and then Save them into another folder for future reference.

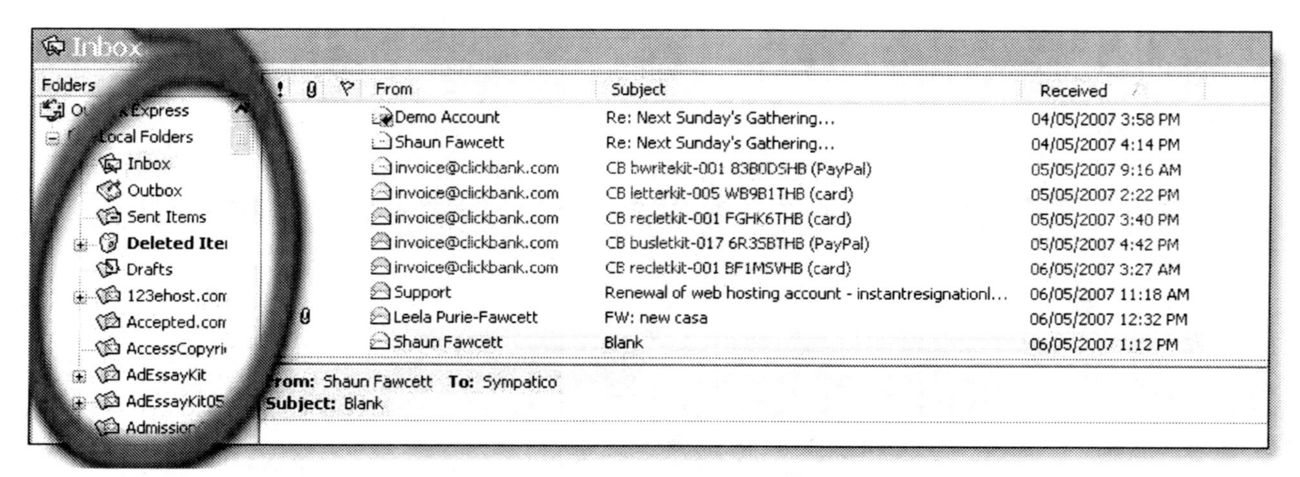

As an example, my list of folders is circled above. This is just the beginning of my list. Over time I have created well over 100 folders, many of those containing numerous sub-folders. In MS-Outlook Express the folders are automatically sorted alphabetically.

To Save an e-mail into any folder, just drag and drop it with your mouse into the desired destination folder.

To do this; in your active folder's main viewing window, left click and HOLD DOWN the left mouse button on the highlighted message that you want to save to another folder.

While continuing to HOLD DOWN on the left mouse button, DRAG the cursor over to the list of folders on the left and STOP on the folder where you want the dragged e-mail saved. Then RELEASE the left mouse button to Save the message into that folder.

How To Create An E-Mail Folder

To create a new folder in which to store e-mails by subject, first left click and highlight the high level folder under which you want the new folder created; then right-click on that to reveal the dropdown menu as per the following screen shot.

For this example, I am creating a new folder at the highest level; Local Folders. On the dropdown menu, click on "New Folder" to activate the Create Folder window. In the space provided, enter the Folder Name for your new folder, as follows:

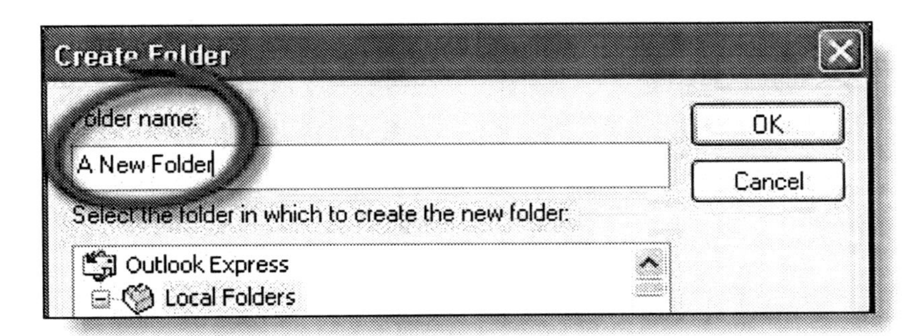

Once you have entered the name of the new folder (e.g. "A New Folder") click the OK Button and the new folder will be created under Local Folders as shown below.

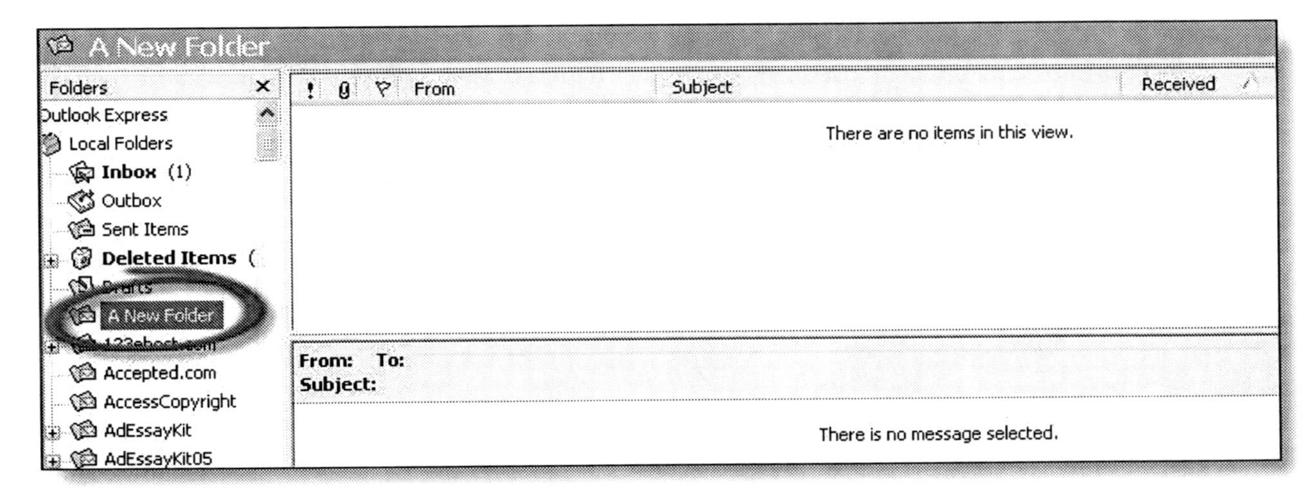

Remember that your new folder will be inserted in the list of folders according to alphabetical order. Accordingly, in this case it has been inserted into the "As".

How To Open An Attachment

An e-mail with an attachment will usually have a paperclip symbol displayed next to it.

To open the attachment directly from your e-mail program, first click on the attachment symbol to the right of the Subject Line in the active folder (i.e., Inbox folder in this example). That will reveal a short dropdown menu with two choices; the first choice will display an icon of the document itself.

To open that document, click on that document icon and the attachment will open into the program with which it is compatible. In this case the document will open directly into MS-Word since it is recognized by the operating system as an MS-Word document.

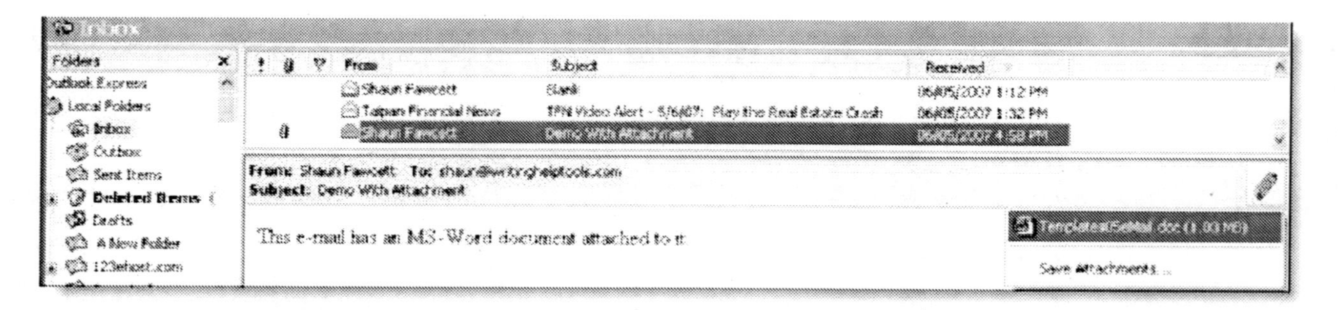

How To Save An Attachment

Click on the second item on the dropdown menu that says "Save Attachments…". The Save Attachments window will open and let you Browse through your folders and navigate to where on your computer you want to save that particular document.

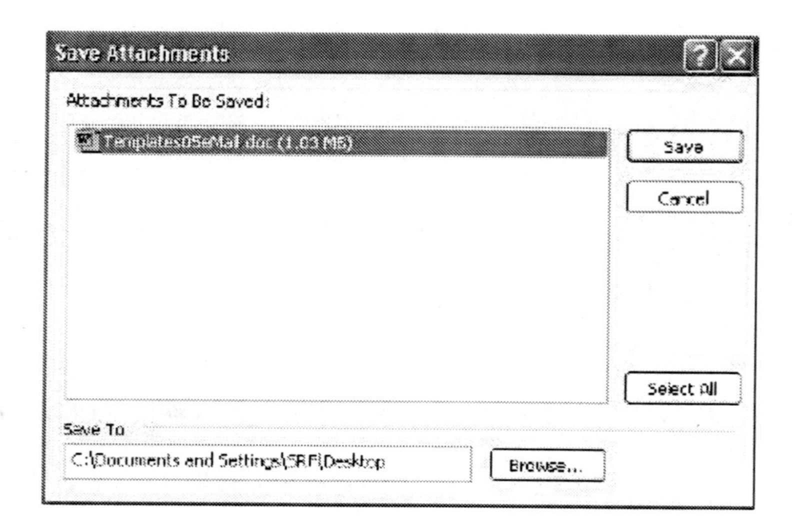

How To Deal With Spam

Spam by e-mail is defined at www.wikipedia.org as "e-mail that is both unsolicited by the recipient and sent in substantively identical form to many recipients." In other words, spam is electronic junk mail. It is estimated by the experts that somewhere between 80% and 85% of all incoming e-mail can be classified as "abusive mail". Just about anyone who has spent even a short period online is familiar with spam.

There are numerous ways to prevent spam from coming into your Inbox, none of them perfect. Nevertheless, with the overwhelming amount of spam being sent these days you MUST have some sort of anti-spam measures in-place.

Spam Filters

The most common way to reduce spam is to use "filters" to screen your e-mail before it arrives in your Inbox. These spam filters check all incoming e-mail and try to identify which incoming e-mail is legitimate and which "appears" to be spam. There are many anti-spam software solutions available. These are usually packaged with anti-virus and anti-spyware software as part of a complete privacy/security solution.

These days, because spam is such a problem, almost all new computer operating systems come pre-loaded with a brand name anti-spam and anti-virus solution. Also, any reputable ISP will offer anti-spam filters that you can easily activate so that any incoming mail that gets filtered out will never reach your Inbox. Online webmail services such as Hotmail, Yahoo Mail, and Google Mail all have filters that you can set up to screen out as much spam as possible.

Setting Up A Spam Filter

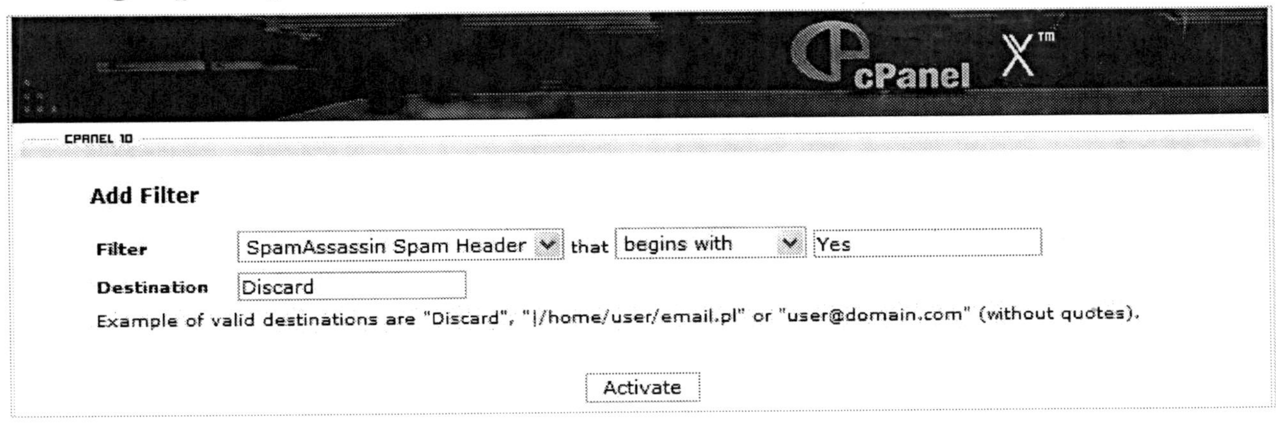

The above is an example of how I can set up spam filters for webmail using software supplied by one of my Web hosting companies. In this case I am telling the filter software to "Discard" all e-mails containing the phrase "SpamAssassin Spam Header" in the Header of the e-mail. That's because I know that the Spam Assassin software that I have set-up to screen my incoming e-mail will place that specific phrase in the header of all e-mails that it detects to be spam.

This is one example. You will need to find out the specific anti-spam filter solution that your ISP offers and use it. Setting these up is a routine, relatively simple process these days. Your ISP will show you exactly what to do.

False Positives

A "false positive" is a legitimate e-mail that, for whatever reason, gets identified by the filter software as spam. The problem with this situation is that this legitimate e-mail that gets identified incorrectly as a spam will never make it into your Inbox so you may never see it. Most anti-spam software filters allow you to get around this problem somewhat by not immediately deleting the e-mail; but instead saving it in a "junk mail" folder so that you can review that folder for false positives later.

Of course, this junk mail folder solution is not perfect since it means you will then have to go to that folder which is 99% full of spam and scan through it looking for any legitimate e-mails that might have been placed there in error.

White Lists

One of the most effective solutions to keep spam out of your Inbox is to create a "whitelist" or "safe list" of acceptable e-mail addresses. This is a list of actual e-mail addresses from which you specify in advance you would like to receive e-mails. Typically, this would be a detailed list of the e-mail addresses of all of your friends, acquaintances, relatives and business contacts.

These are useful anti-spam lists but they are not perfect since when you set them up there is no way to be sure that you have listed the e-mail address of every possible legitimate sender of e-mail. Also, over time you will acquire additional legitimate contacts that will not be on your list until you remember to put them there. In addition, whenever one of your white listed approved senders changes their e-mail address you will have to revise your whitelist/safelist right away or risk losing important e-mails from valued contacts. This is another effective but imperfect anti-spam solution.

Creating a Whitelist Or Safelist

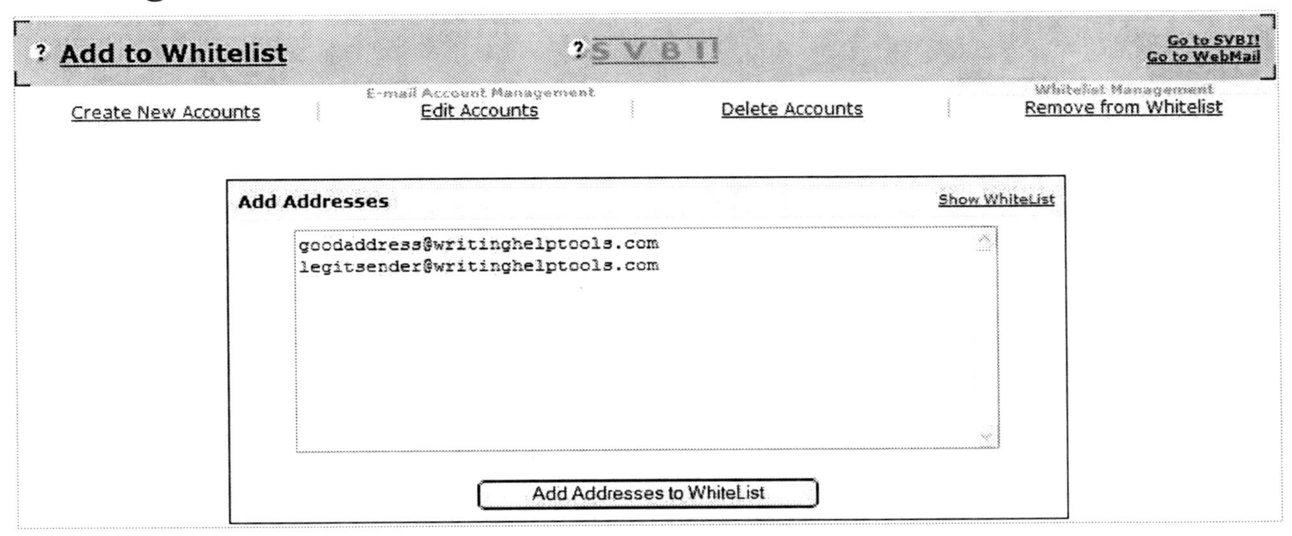

Above is an example of whitelist creation software that I use at one of my Web hosting companies for screening my webmail. As you can see, it is simply a process of entering a list of "trusted" e-mail addresses from which you agree in advance to receive e-mail. E-mail from addresses that are not included on my whitelist/safelist will either be further screened using other criteria or will be routed to the junk folder immediately.

Your ISP company will have software in-place that will allow you to quickly and easily set up your own whitelist. Just ask them how to do it.

Spam Management in Hotmail

Hotmail is a good case to look at in terms of the options they give their users to protect them against spam. They call it "Junk E-Mail Protection" but they are referring to what most others call spam.

Hotmail's main forms of protection are the same as discussed above: e-mail filters and safe lists. In addition, they offer certain spam management options and the ability to block e-mail from specific address and/or domains. Click on the Mail tab to see them.

Spam Management Options - Hotmail

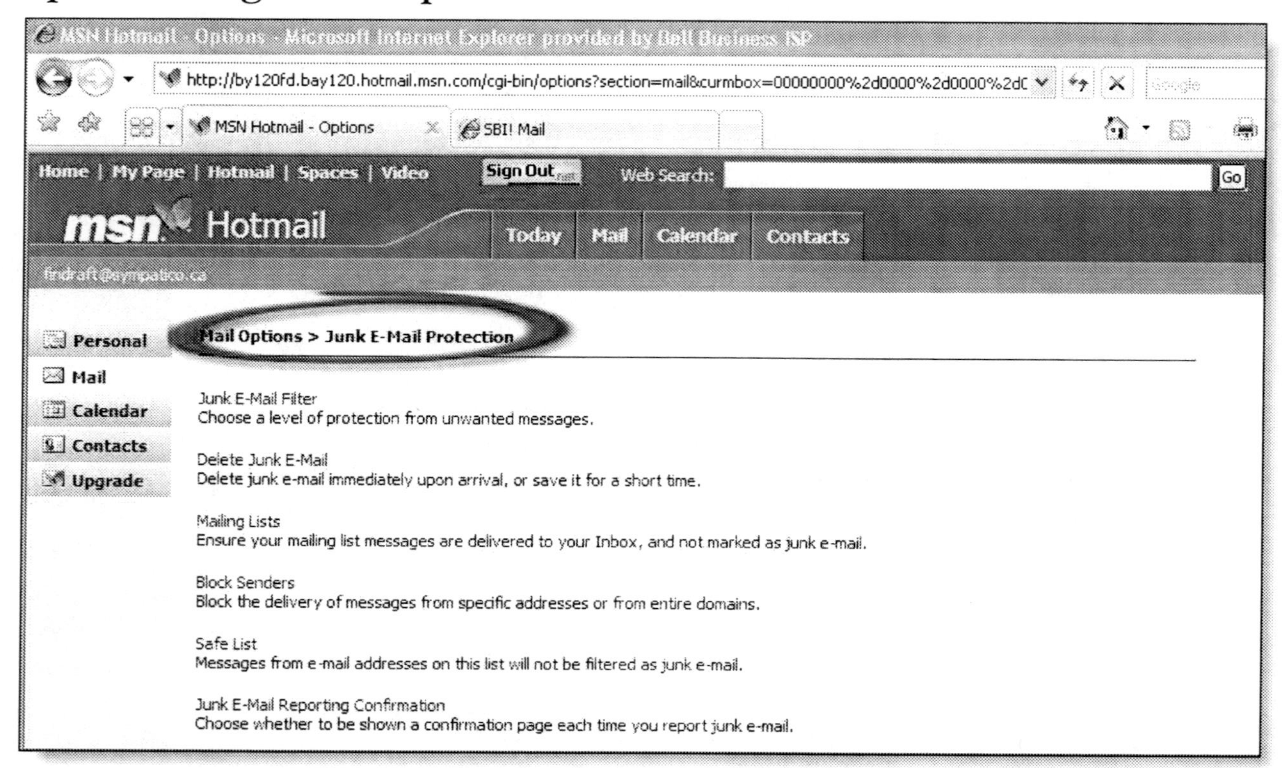

The purpose of the above screen shot is to show you the list of Hotmail spam management options. If you are a Hotmail user I urge you to check these out further and set them up to suit your own preferences.

Whether you use Hotmail or another service doesn't really matter. These days, all major Webmail services provide very similar capabilities.

An Anti-Spam Pre-Screener

A few years ago I came across an excellent tool that allows me to quickly pre-screen all e-mails that slip through the various e-mail filters and still try to get into my Inbox. The program is called Mailwasher. When I initiate the program, Mailwasher goes to all of my e-mail accounts (e.g. ISP servers) and downloads the headers ONLY for those e-mails, and then lists those headers in an easy to review list that I can quickly review and check-off which e-mails I want to download and which I want to delete.

I wouldn't do without Mailwasher. You can check it out here:
http://firetrust.com/en/download/mailwasher-pro

E-Mail Etiquette

You would be amazed at some of the pure gibberish that arrives in my e-mailbox on a regular basis.

For some reason, many people seem to think that because they aren't dealing directly with another (or as directly as face-to-face or via telephone), or not writing in their own hand (as in a personal letter), all forms of civility and basic respect for the other person (i.e. the recipient), and the English language, can go out the proverbial window.

Not true! Writing e-mails is still writing, and both **the language and the recipient still deserve your respect.**

Since the Internet was founded, a few unofficial, yet imperative, standard conventions have evolved over time with respect to the sending of e-mails. **This norm for online behavior is often referred to as "Netiquette".**

The following passages were first drafted for my book entitled "*Internet Basics without fear! Quick-Start Guide for Becoming Internet Friendly In Just a Few Easy Steps*", Revised Ed., Final Draft!, Montreal, March 2000. I later published them in an article titled *"E-Mail 101: The Dos and Don'ts*". Following is a revised and updated version of that article.

E-Mail 101: The Dos and Don'ts

DO... Use A Descriptive Subject Line

There is nothing more annoying than receiving e-mails in your e-Inbox with no heading, or a heading that does not explain what the contents of the message is all about. The only thing that can make your message stand out in the recipient's Inbox is a unique Subject Line that states what your message is all about.

When one receives multiple messages every day, the subject-line is important when reviewing and prioritizing e-mail that is in one's Inbox. Also, if you include a descriptive title, your message is almost guaranteed to be read before the ones with blank or meaningless titles.

Tip: *I even revise the Subject Line when I am sending a Reply, in order to reflect the essence of my response. This is especially useful if it's one of those e-mails that travels back and forth 3 or 4 times. Often, there is little relationship between the point of the first message and the later ones. So, try revising the Subject Line slightly each time to reflect the content of your current message.**(See page 53).*

DO... Use Opening and Closing Salutations

Some people have forgotten that e-mail is interpersonal communication between human beings. Basic civility still applies.

There is nothing much more impersonal than receiving an e-mail that doesn't at least say "Hello..." or "Hi..." for the opening; and "Regards..." or "Thanks..." or "Take care..." or "All the best...", or something similar as the closing.

We can't personally sign the note by hand anymore, but we can surely personalize it a little bit by at least typing in the recipient's name in the greeting salutation and wishing them the best when we sign off.

DO... Use Capital Letters Sparingly

The use of all-caps is shunned on the Internet. It's called SHOUTING. Nevertheless, every once in a while a word or two typed in capitals for particular emphasis is ok, but avoid overdoing it.

Tip: *Cutesy little smiles and similar symbols, known as emoticons, should also be used sparingly. :-) I advise you not to use these symbols at all in business e-mails, unless the recipient is a friend or well-known to you. Just as with business letters, the principle underlying business e-mails is: clear and concise businesslike communication with a minimum of clutter. '-)*

DO... Check Spelling, Grammar, and Format

Make a point to ensure that your e-mail is relatively readable. It doesn't have to be a work of art, but at least respect the basic rules of spelling and grammar. Most e-mail programs have a spell-checker option. Use it. (See page 44).

Tip: *For better readability, break your e-mail into short 1,2, or 3 sentence paragraphs with a blank line between paragraphs. (i.e. double hard-return).*

DO... Watch Out For "E-Mail Rage"

Many an e-mail has been composed and sent when a person was in an angry or upset state (referred to as "flaming"). Many people have lived to regret these indiscretions in the cold sober light of the next hour, or the next day. Remember, whenever the Send button has been clicked, your e-mail is gone.

Tip: *When you compose an e-mail while in an "upset state", it is always a good idea to save it as a draft for an hour or two and then read it over carefully at least once before sending it, just to make sure you are communicating what you really want to, in a clear and respectful way.*

DON'T... Forward Junk Mail To Others

From time to time, people to whom we have given our e-mail address will have momentary lapses in judgment (yes, even friends and family) and will forward "junk mail" to you.

These are often long rambling stories, urban myths, scraps of wisdom, chain letters, collections of jokes, or such, that are prevalent around the Net.

This is the equivalent of opening your regular mail box at home and finding it loaded with unsolicited and unwanted promotional letters and advertising flyers. Would you forward regular junk mail to your friends or family? Do you? I didn't think so.

When you receive one of these in your Inbox, DO NOT forward it on to someone else. Kill it then and there. This kind of unsolicited junk mail is known as "spam", and is definitely not acceptable on the Net.

If a friend or acquaintance sends one to you, politely e-mail them back asking if they would please be kind enough to remove your name from their distribution list for that type of item. Gently explain that you are already inundated with this "type" of unsolicited e-mail. Usually, they will take the hint and accommodate you.

DON'T... Think That E-Mail Is Instantaneous

Believe it or not, e-mail is NOT as reliable as a telephone call when it comes to timely communication!

The Internet is a loosely connected network of computers and telecommunications equipment owned, operated, and managed by many independent companies, institutions, and government organizations. Your e-mail must often travel a complex and circuitous route to get to its destination. For example, if someone schedules maintenance on a computer or a piece of equipment on the network that your e-mail must pass through, your message may be delayed and you won't even know it.

Also, who is to guarantee that the intended recipient even checks their e-mail regularly? Many people only check their e-mail every few days. So, if your communication is urgent, use the standard telephone. It is still the only way to be absolutely sure that a message has been received at a particular point in time.

DON'T... Forget To Check Your E-Mail Regularly

There is nothing more frustrating than sending an e-mail to someone and then having them tell you on the telephone a week later that they haven't seen your message because the last time they checked their e-mail was a week ago! If you want people to take your e-mails seriously, make sure that you take theirs seriously too. So, check your e-mail regularly; at least every two or three days.

The bottom line to all of this is simple. Remember that e-mail is just another form of interpersonal communication. People deserve the same amount of respect and civility as you would give them in a telephone call or a regular letter.

As I mentioned above, the general quality of e-mails sent by many people needs a lot of improvement just to facilitate basic communication. I'm not talking about e-mail writers becoming professional copywriters or anything like that. I'm talking about using some very basic standards for spelling and grammar.

Oh, and let's not forget, some basic manners too!

Inappropriate E-Mails - Samples

Just to make my point; **below are verbatim texts** of a few e-mails received at my writinghelp-central.com website over the past few years. (Names and addresses have been omitted to protect the guilty!).

Inappropriate E-Mail 1

> i fuond your tips useful on doing a cv as i need one for work eperience as my current one was rubbish

Inappropriate E-Mail 2

> OK, I HAVE A QUESTION THAT YOU MIGHT HELP ME ON, I HAVE BEEN A WEB USER FOR THE PAST FEW MONTHS AND I CAN NOT SEEM TO ACCESS THE PAGE WHERE YOU CAN ACTUALLY WRITE LETTERS, DOCUMENTS, ETC. I HAVE WENT TO WEB BUILDER HOWEVER, I DO NOT WANT TO USE THE COLORS THAT THEY PROVIDE FOR YOU AND WELL I AM STUCK. I NEED TO TYPE THINGS AND I CAN'T DO IT AT WORK, FOR I WOULD GET INTO TROUBLE, THAT IS ONE REASON WHY I BOUGHT THIS WEBTV SO THAT I COULD USE THE PRINTER TO WRITE LETTERS, ETC. THANK YOU FOR REGARDING THIS AND I HOPE THAT I HEAR SOMETHING FROM YOU SOON.

Inappropriate E-Mail 3

> Cld you send me a mssge from yr proper address the one yu want me to use, That way I can save it.

Inappropriate E-Mail 4

> great i am a looking at working as a private investigator tried before but failed due to not being able to market my company some good ideas thank you.

Inappropriate E-Mail 5

> I fgot to tell you that I'm going out of twn on holiday July 27- Sug 3 so will not be able to visit L. then, in case you want to do that."

The samples above are just a tiny sampling of the **<u>thousands</u>** of similar e-mails that I have received over the years.

Seriously, there really is no excuse for sending the above quality of e-mails to anyone. I can tell you, the moment I get one of these I am in no hurry to reply. In fact, I find such messages to be insulting.

If you author e-mails like those above, just imagine how you must appear to the recipient. How about; sloppy, unprofessional, rude, and disrespectful, to name a few.

Do you really want to give people this impression? I doubt it.

Appropriate E-Mails - Samples

The following are a few examples of what I consider to be appropriately written e-mails for a few typical situations.

They are cordial and respectful, and use understandable English that gets the message across in a clear and concise fashion.

Appropriate E-Mail 1 – Answer To An Inquiry

Dear Pamela,

Thanks for your kind comments. The next version of the site will be even better. In the near future, we will be incorporating many more samples into it, as well as some additional resource links.

When the new version is ready we will drop you a line.

Thanks again, and come back soon.

John Smith

Appropriate E-Mail 2 – Reply To A Friend or Acquaintance

Hi Peter,

A copy of the latest edition of the magazine will be mailed to you tomorrow. The article I did on Jill Hennessy is on the cover of this one. If you haven't received it in a week or so, please get back to me and I will follow-up.

Take care, and do keep in touch.

Shaun

Appropriate E-Mail 3 – Question To A Company

Hello Amazon People,

Three months ago, I ordered a book from you people entitled "Internet Basics For Beginners". I have not yet received that book. The order number you gave me is LX9872543. Please check on this and get back to me ASAP.

Thanks very much.

Miranda Wheeler

Appropriate E-mail 4 – Cover/Explanatory E-Mail

Hello Everyone,

Attached to this is the latest draft of the Environics proposal. It is pretty well in final form except that the graphics for the figures have not been inserted to save disk space and transmission time.

I would appreciate your comments by tomorrow noon at the latest. That should give me just enough time to add your changes and then finalize the package before Wednesday 10:00 a.m. submission deadline.

Even if you have nil comments, could you please just send me a quick reply to this stating such.Thanks for your help and cooperation.

Frank Marchmount

As demonstrated above, writing a readable and respectful e-mail that clearly communicates your message is not all that difficult.

How To Reply To E-Mails Appropriately

It seems that a lot of people are confused about how to best reply to an e-mail. This is an important point, especially when you want to reply to specific points or issues mentioned in the senders message to you.

I have found that the most effective way to reply to an e-mail is to address each of the sender's comments or questions separately. I think that the best way to show you this is by example, as follows:

Typical Request E-Mail – Sample

Hello Shaun,

I want to buy one of your writing kits but I'm not sure which one would be best for me. I own my own business and I am looking for something to improve the quality of my business correspondence in general. When I look at your Kits I'm not sure if I should buy the Home Writing Kit, the Business Letter Kit, or the Letter Writing Kit. Please help! Also, how much?

Jackie Marsden

Ideal Response To Request E-Mail - Sample

Hello Jackie,

Thanks for your request. I'll address your points below.

>When I look at your Kits I'm not sure if I should buy the Home Writing Kit, the Business >Letter Kit, or your Letter Writing Kit.
They would all help with business letter writing but if your focus is 100% business I suggest the Business Letter Kit for you. The other two are more general purpose in nature.

>Also, how much?
All three sell for the same price of $29.97; so that should make that part of the decision easy.

Thanks and all the best,

Shaun Fawcett

As you can see, all I did was copy and paste the sender's relevant question phrases into the top part of my reply e-mail and then answered them one point at a time. (For more information on How To Copy and Paste, go to page 15).

This approach can be used for any type of e-mail; business or personal. I highly recommend it because it ensures a very specific point-by-point response, and then nothing gets missed. (See page 53).

Working With Hotmail

As mentioned earlier, Hotmail is one of the most popular free Webmail services online. The other two popular services are Yahoo! Mail and Google Mail.

Because Hotmail is one of the most widely-used Webmail services, this chapter presents the basics of using Hotmail. Even if you use a different Webmail service it will still be useful to review this section since; aside from a different look, feel, and color scheme, theses services are very similar to work with from a practical perspective. (See page 81).

Hotmail Sign-In

If you already have a hotmail account, just enter your e-mail address and password into the appropriate fields in the sign-in box as per below.

Hotmail Sign-In Screen

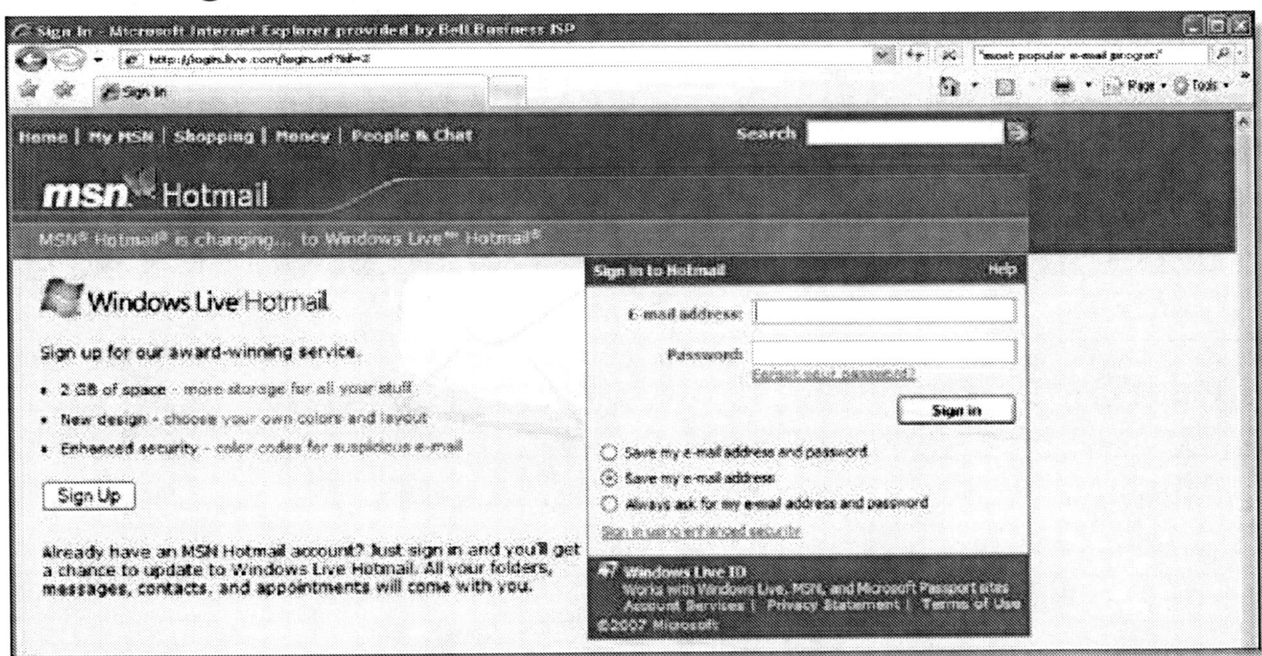

If you haven't yet registered with hotmail just click on the "Sign Up" button on the lower left portion of the page and follow the instructions.

To sign up for either of the two other popular services, click on the appropriate link:
https://login.yahoo.com/config/mail?.intl=us
https://www.google.com/accounts/NewAccount

Once you have signed in at Hotmail you will be taken to the following "Today" screen.

Opening Mail Status Screen

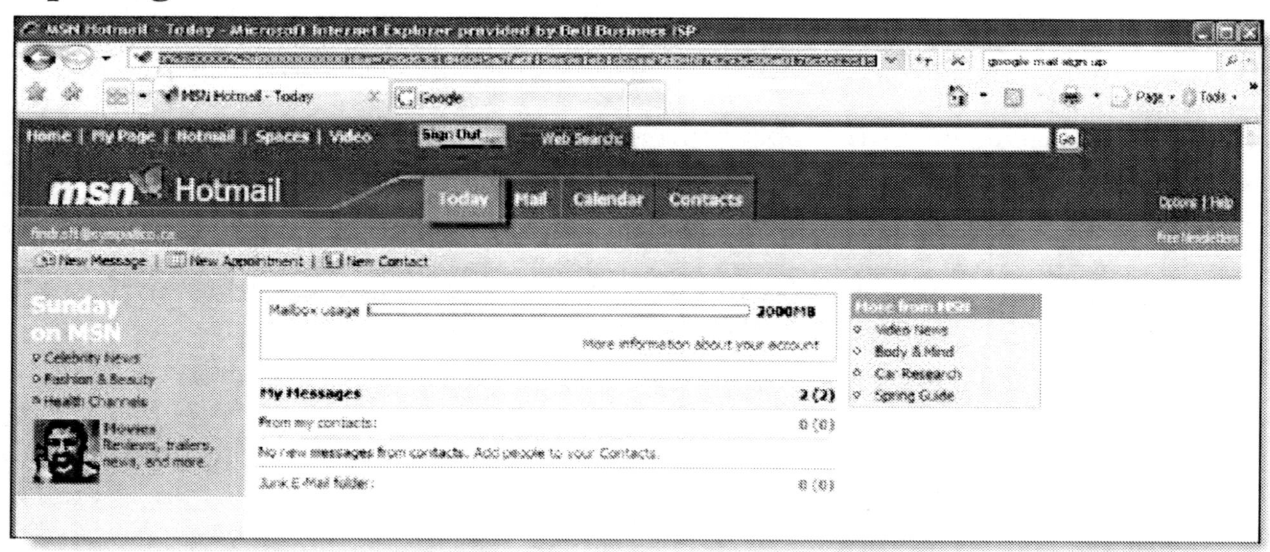

If you look to the right of "My Messages" you can see that it indicates that there are two (2) messages waiting to be read in my Inbox. To go to your Inbox to review those messages you can either click on the "My Messages" hyperlink (above) or on the "Mail" tab as highlighted below.

Review Mail/Inbox Screen

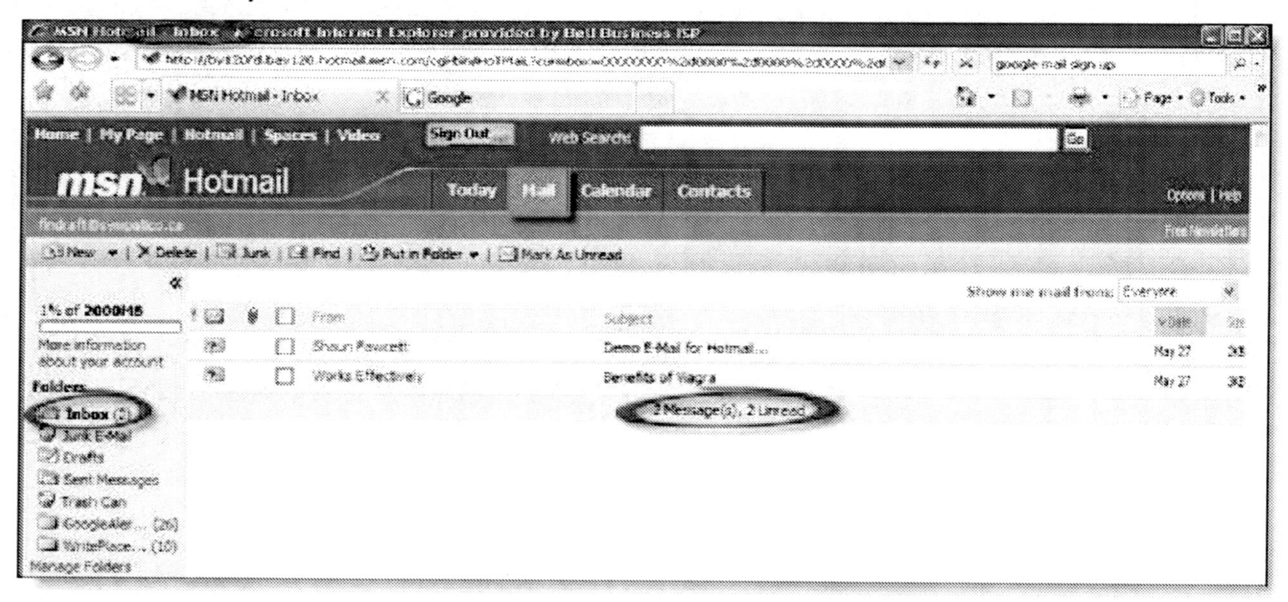

Notice that you can tell that you are in your Inbox by looking at the top of screen status bar as highlighted above. It will also be the bolded folder in the list of folders on the left, also as highlighted above.

To read an e-mail in the Inbox click on the Name shown in the "From" field. So, to read the first of the two e-mails in the above Inbox click on "Shaun Fawcett"; my name is listed in the "From" field since it is a demo e-mail that I sent to myself.

Read E-Mail Screen

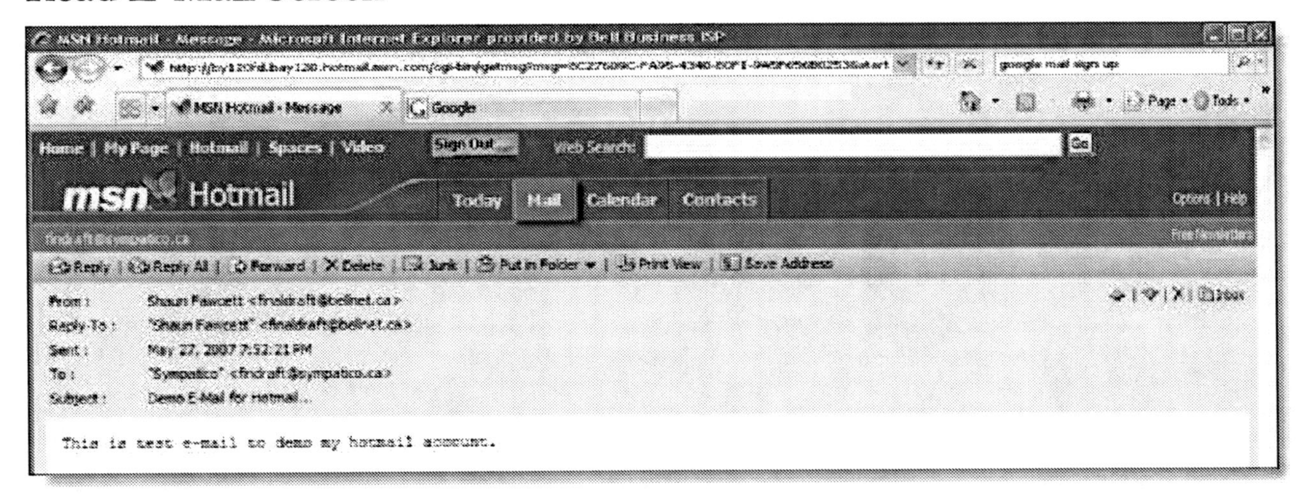

To take any kind of action on the current e-mail that is displayed, click on the appropriate function on the E-Mail Action Toolbar as shown below:

E-Mail Action Toolbar

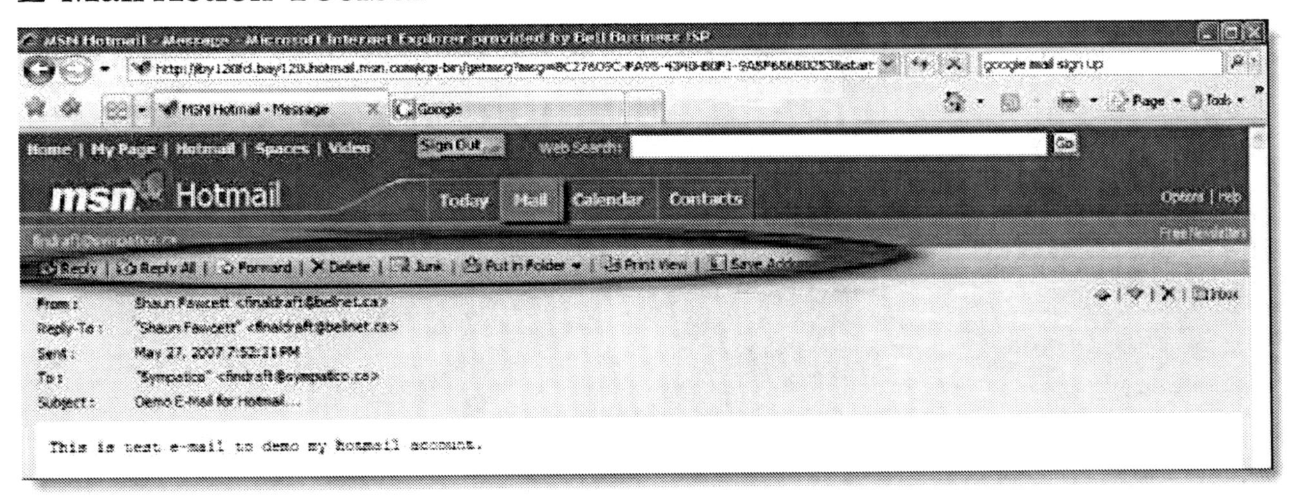

This E-Mail Action Toolbar comprises all of the typical e-mail toolbar action functions such as: Reply, Reply All, Forward, Delete, Junk, Print, etc.

If you are unsure as to what any of these functions means, please go back and review these in the earlier section on Composing and Sending E-Mails in MS-Outlook Express on page 43. These functions are generic, regardless of the software you are using.

Composing and Sending E-Mails In Hotmail

To Compose a new e-mail, first click on the "Today" tab which displays your overall e-mail status at the current time. Then click on the "New Message" button as per below.

Today Status Tab

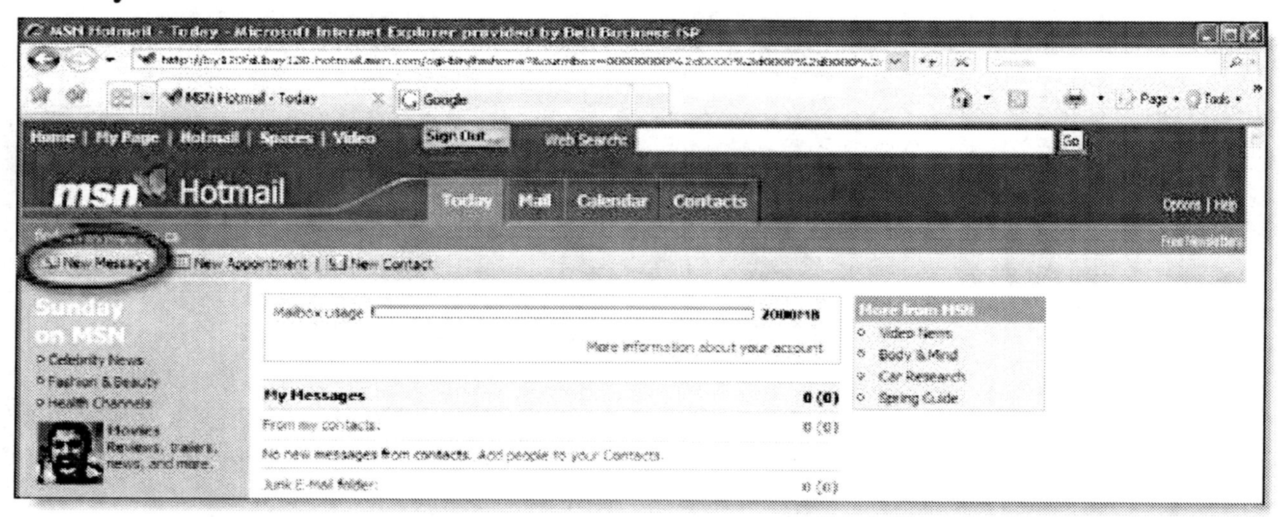

Clicking on the "New Message" button will open the Compose E-Mail Screen as shown below. This is the window where you enter: the "To:" e-mail info for the addressee(s), the "Subject:", and the text of your message in the fields provided for such.

Compose E-Mail Screen

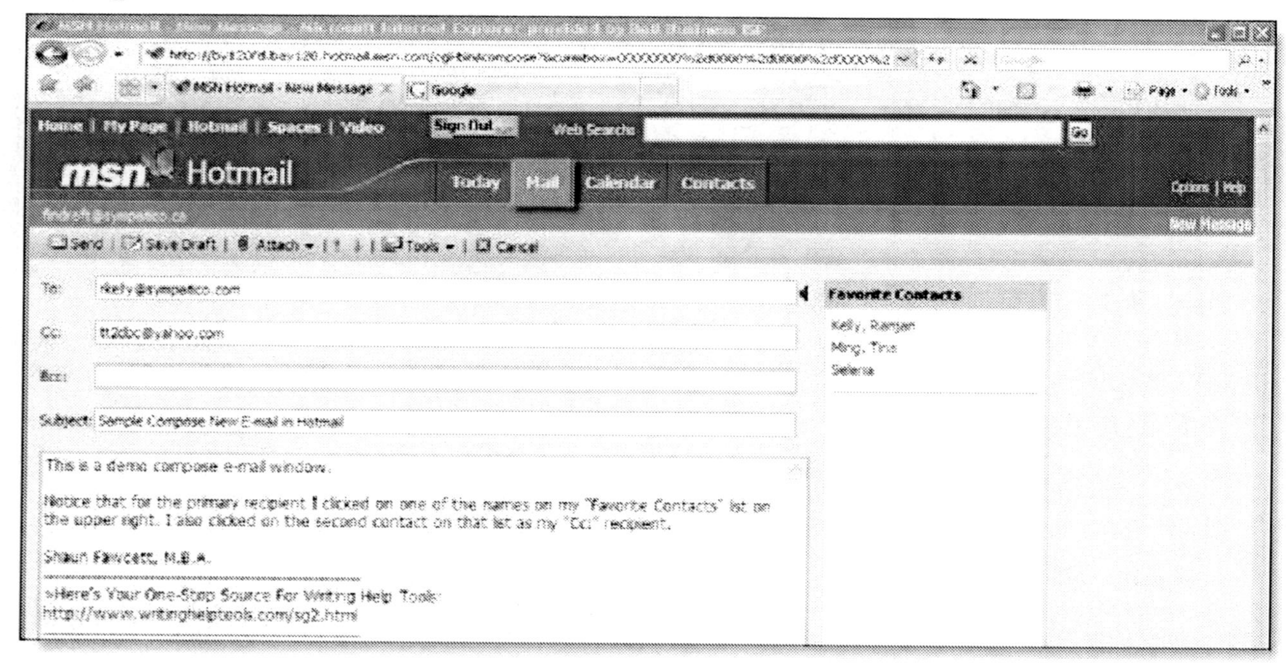

When complete, click on the 'Send" button on the E-Mail Action Toolbar.

Replying To E-Mails In Hotmail

Because these functions are generic, I will not go through all of them here for Hotmail. For example; to Reply to the current e-mail that is open in your Inbox click on the "Reply" button on the E-mail Action Toolbar to reveal The Compose E-mail Screen:

Reply (Compose E-Mail) Screen In Hotmail

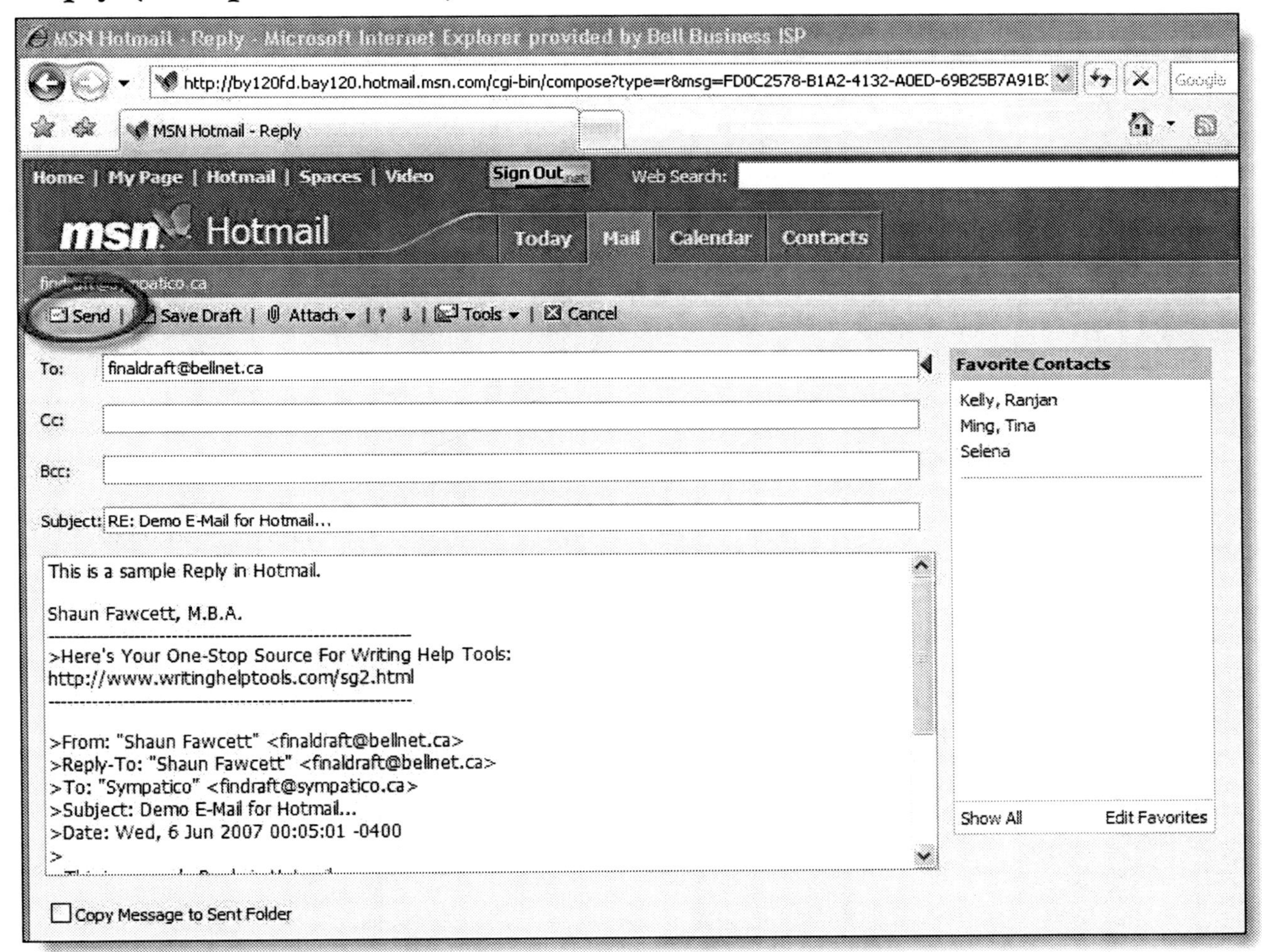

Hotmail automatically inserts the original e-mail to which you are replying at the bottom of your new e-mail. In addition, it automatically inserts your "Signature" if you have specified one in E-Mail Options mode. Also, by checking the box at the lower-left corner you can Save a copy of your outgoing e-mail in your "Sent" folder.

Once you have added your Reply in the text window as per above, click on the "Send" button on the E-Mail Toolbar. When you click on the "Send" button, Hotmail sends your e-mail immediately.

It will also give you the option to add the recipient of the outgoing e-mail to your "Favorite Contacts" list as shown below. To Add the current recipient, checkmark the appropriate box on the right and then click on the Add Button.

Add Contacts Window

Of course, if it finds the recipient already on your contacts list it won't display this box.

Sending Attachments In Hotmail

To add an attachment such as a document or a photo, click on the "Attach" button on the E-Mail Action Toolbar of the Compose E-Mail window. For example, see that Toolbar near the top of the Reply Screen on the previous page.

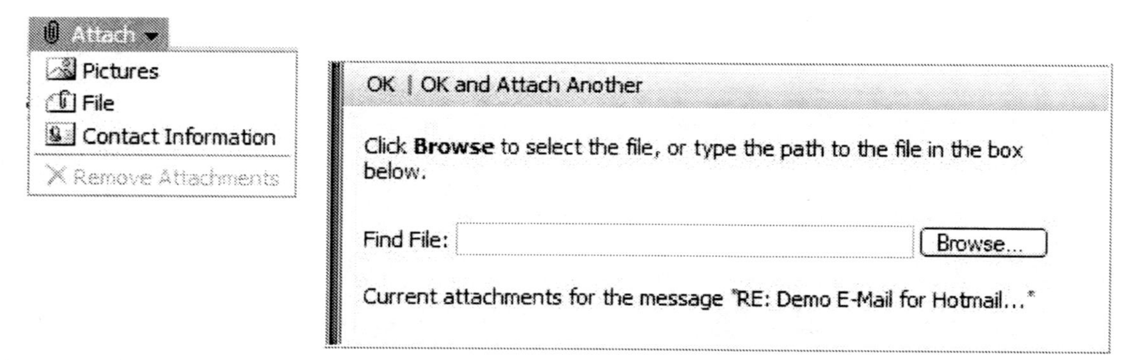

Clicking on the "Attach" button will reveal a dropdown menu where you can choose the type of attachment, as per above left. Click on the appropriate item in the menu list. The window on the right will open so you can "Browse" through the files on your hard drive. Once you have arrived at the correct file, click on the "OK" button in the top left corner of the window after which you will be returned to the Compose window.

Selecting E-Mail Options In Hotmail

To select various e-mail option settings in Hotmail, first click on the "Mail" tab and then click on the "Options" tab on the right, as highlighted below:

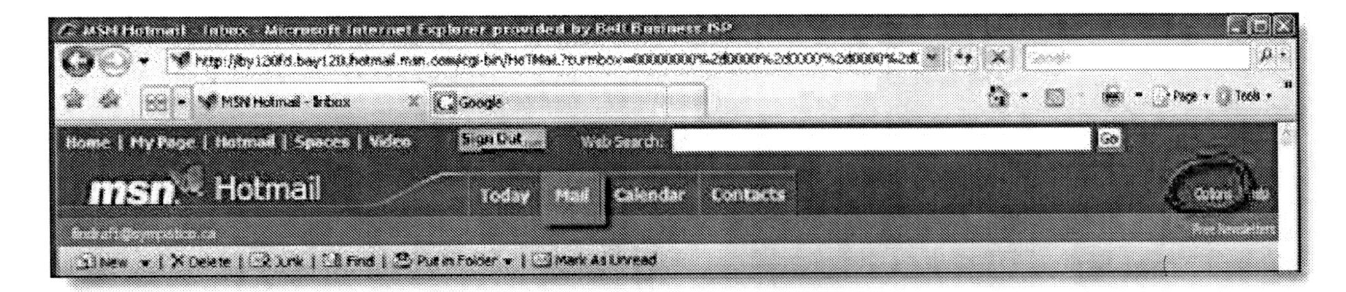

Clicking on the "Options" tab will open a special Options window, as follows:

MSN Hotmail – Mail Options Window

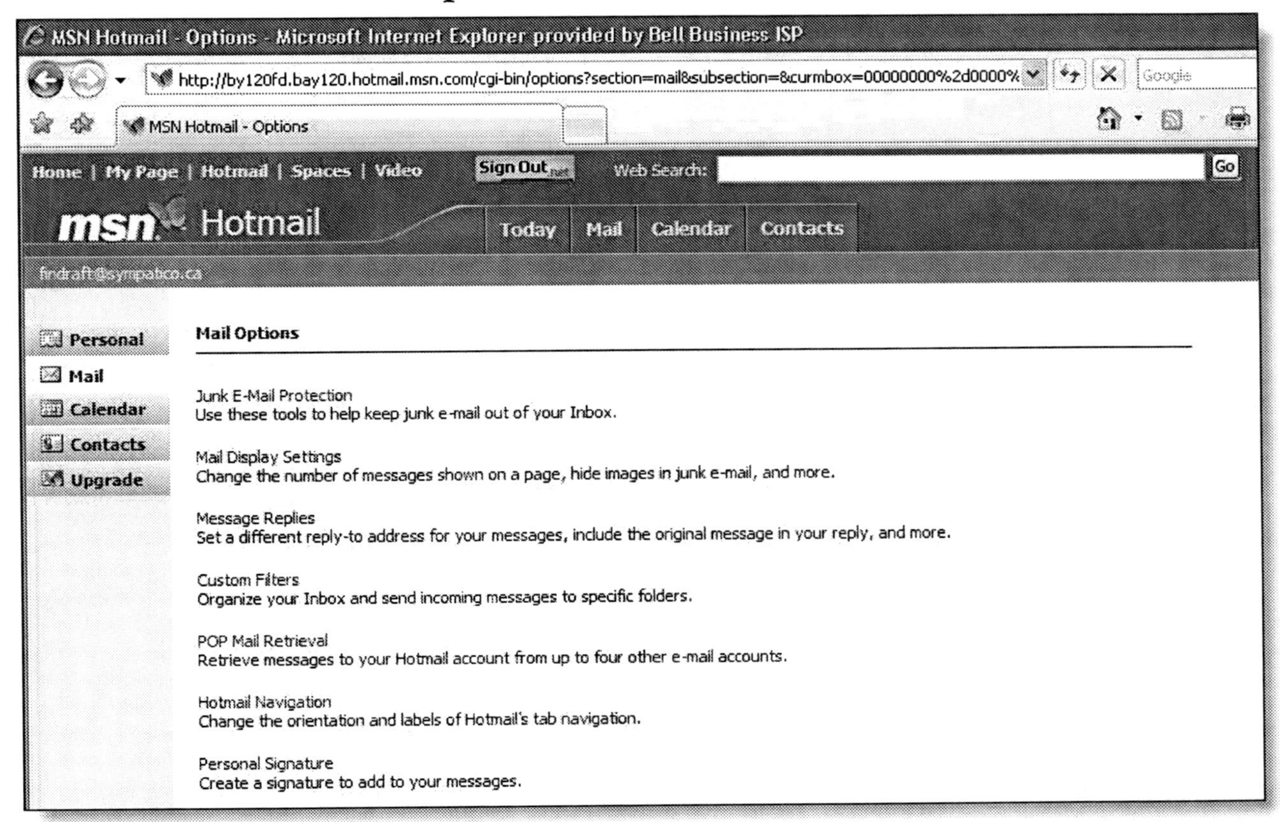

I will not go into the details of any of these options here. The only one of these that I have mentioned on previous pages is the "Personal Signature" setting. To find out more about each one, simply click on it and explore the possibilities. Most beginners don't really need to change these from the default settings.

Working With Yahoo! Mail

Yahoo! Mail is the most popular Webmail service used by subscribers to my free writing help newsletters. More than one-third of my current subscribers use Yahoo! Mail.

Because of it's popularity I have decided to include a section here that covers the basics of using Yahoo! Mail. As I have stated before, even if you use a different Webmail service it will still be helpful to review this section since, aside from a different look, feel and color scheme, these services are very similar in terms of functionality.

Yahoo! Mail Sign-In

If you already have a Yahoo! ID, just enter it with your password into the appropriate fields as shown below.

Yahoo! Mail Sign-In Screen

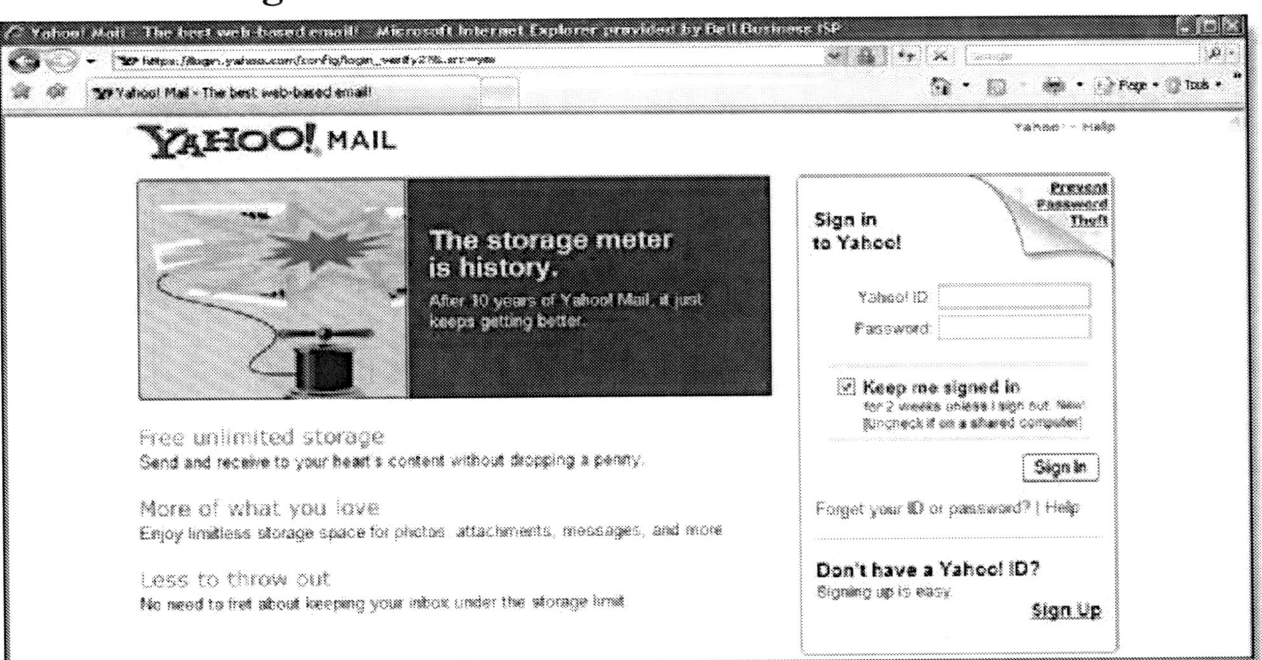

If you haven't yet registered with Yahoo! Click on the "Don't Have A Yahoo ID?" Sign Up link on the bottom right of the sign-in screen.

To sign up for either of the two other popular services, click on the appropriate link:
http://get.live.com/mail/options
https://www.google.com/accounts/NewAccount

Once you have signed in at Yahoo! Mail you will be taken to the following screen:

Opening Mail Status/Review Screen

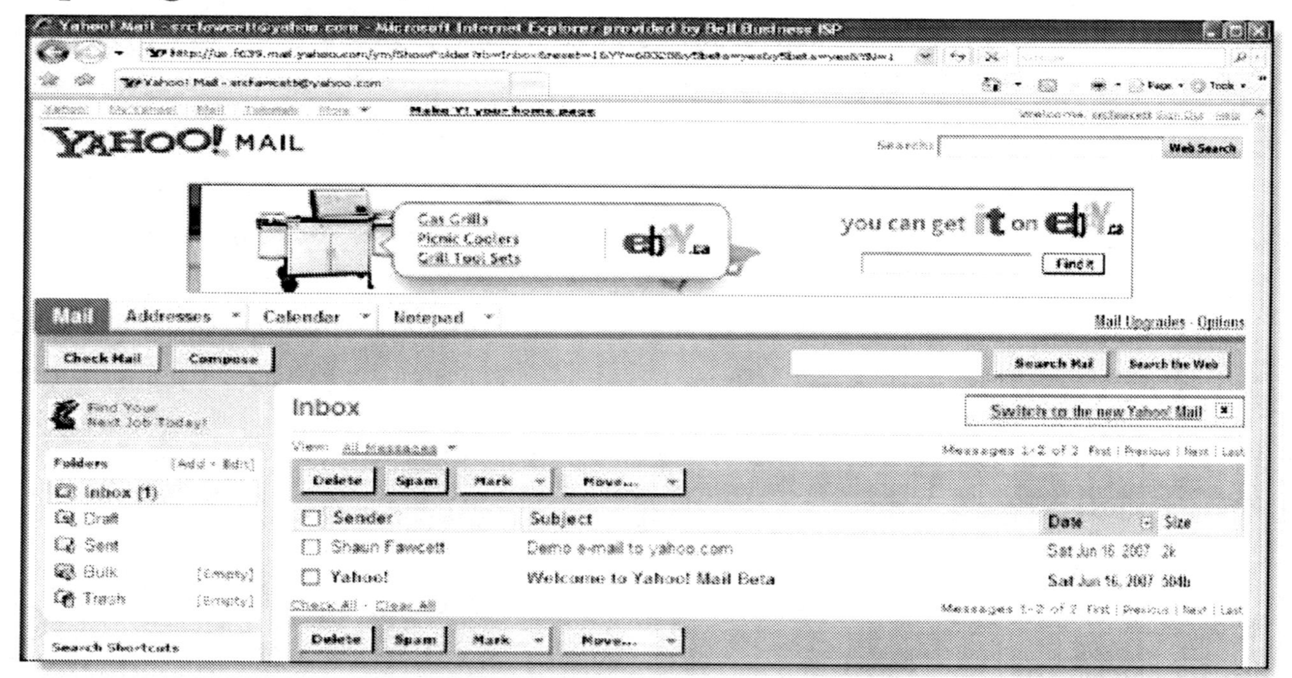

The above screen lists the messages currently in your Inbox. To read a message just click on the hyperlinked Subject of that e-mail to reveal the Read E-mail Screen.

Read E-Mail Screen

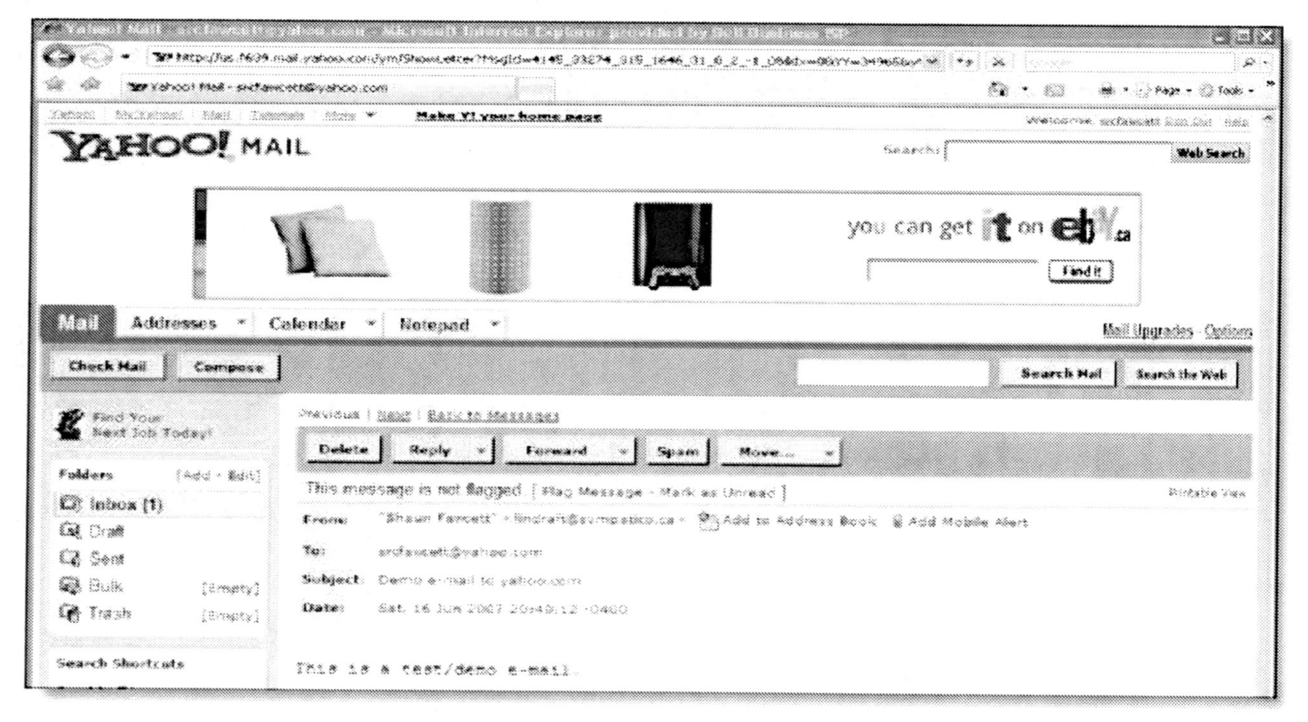

Take note of the relatively large advertisements displayed near the top of the previous two screen shots. This is one of the hidden costs of a "free" e-mail service.

To take any kind of action on the e-mail that you are currently viewing, click on the appropriate function on the E-mail Action Toolbar as shown below:

E-Mail Action Toolbar

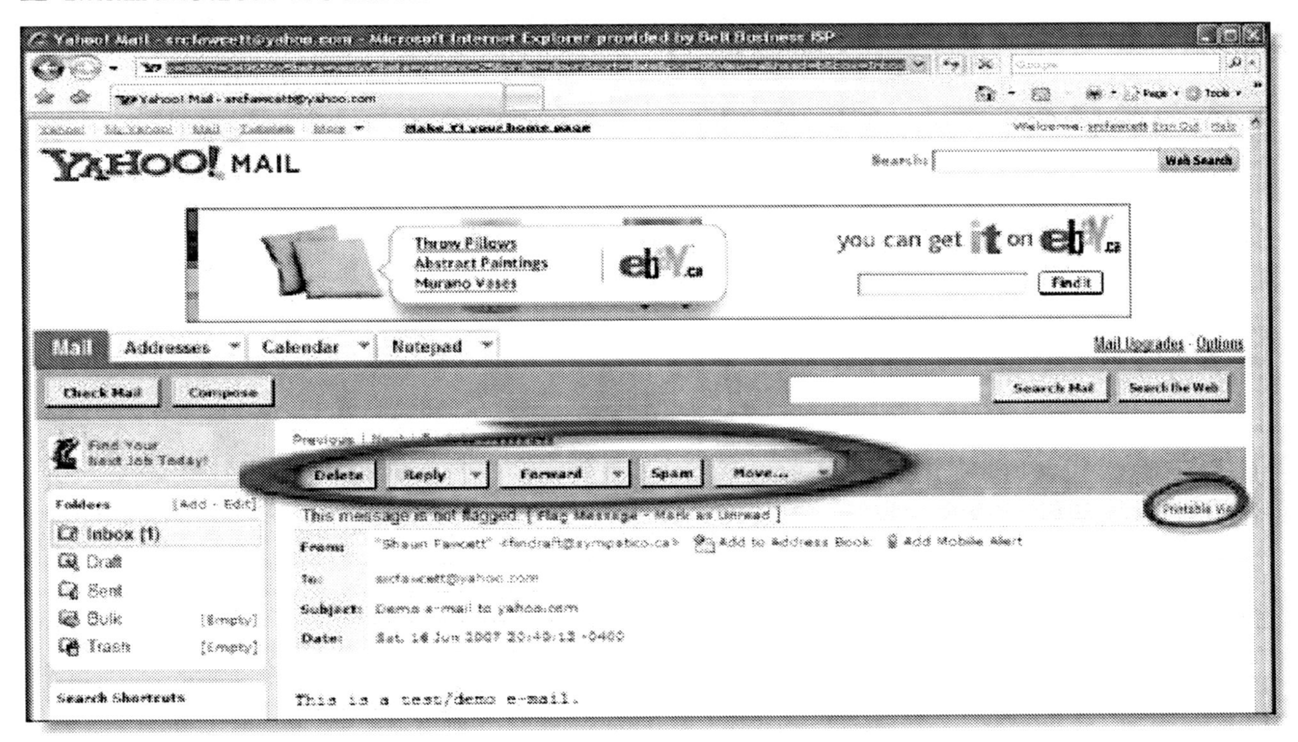

The E-Mail Action Toolbar comprises all of the typical e-mail toolbar functions including: Delete, Reply, Forward, Spam, and Move. Notice that the button for the Print view is on the extreme right.

If you are unsure about what any of these functions does, please go back to the earlier section on Composing and Sending E-Mails in MS Outlook Express on page 43. These functions are mostly generic in nature, regardless of the software you are using.

The one exception to this is the prominence of the Spam Button on the Yahoo! E-Mail Action Toolbar. This opens a new window in which one can designate an e-mail as spam and report the sender as a spammer if desired.

Composing E-Mails In Yahoo! Mail

To compose a new e-mail, first click on the main "Mail" tab which displays your Welcome Message and Inbox status. Then click on the "Compose" button as per the screen shot below.

Mail Status Screen

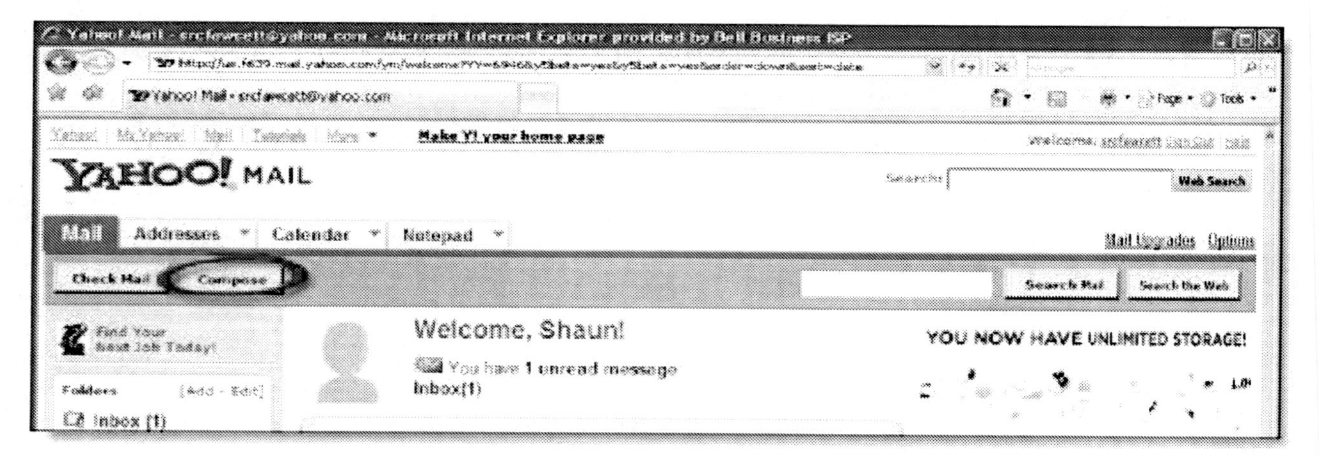

When the Compose E-Mail Screen opens as shown below, you just enter the appropriate info such as the "To:" e-mail address, the "Subject:" heading text, and the actual text of the e-mail.

Compose E-Mail Screen

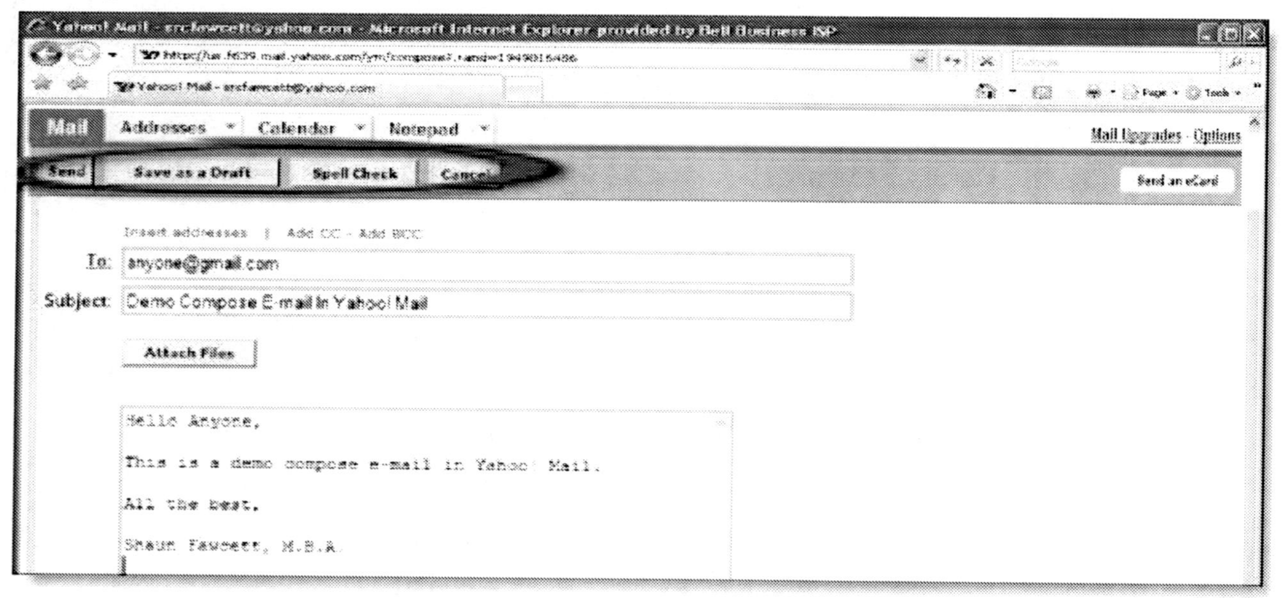

Note that at this point you can also do a few other things at this stage such as Spell Check and Save As Draft using the buttons highlighted above. When you have done everything, simply click on the "Send" button on the left end of the Action Toolbar.

Replying To E-Mails In Yahoo! Mail

To Reply to the current e-mail that is open in your Inbox, click on the 'Reply" button on the E-mail Action Toolbar to reveal the Compose E-Mail Screen. (See page 84).

Reply (Compose E-Mail) Screen In Yahoo! Mail

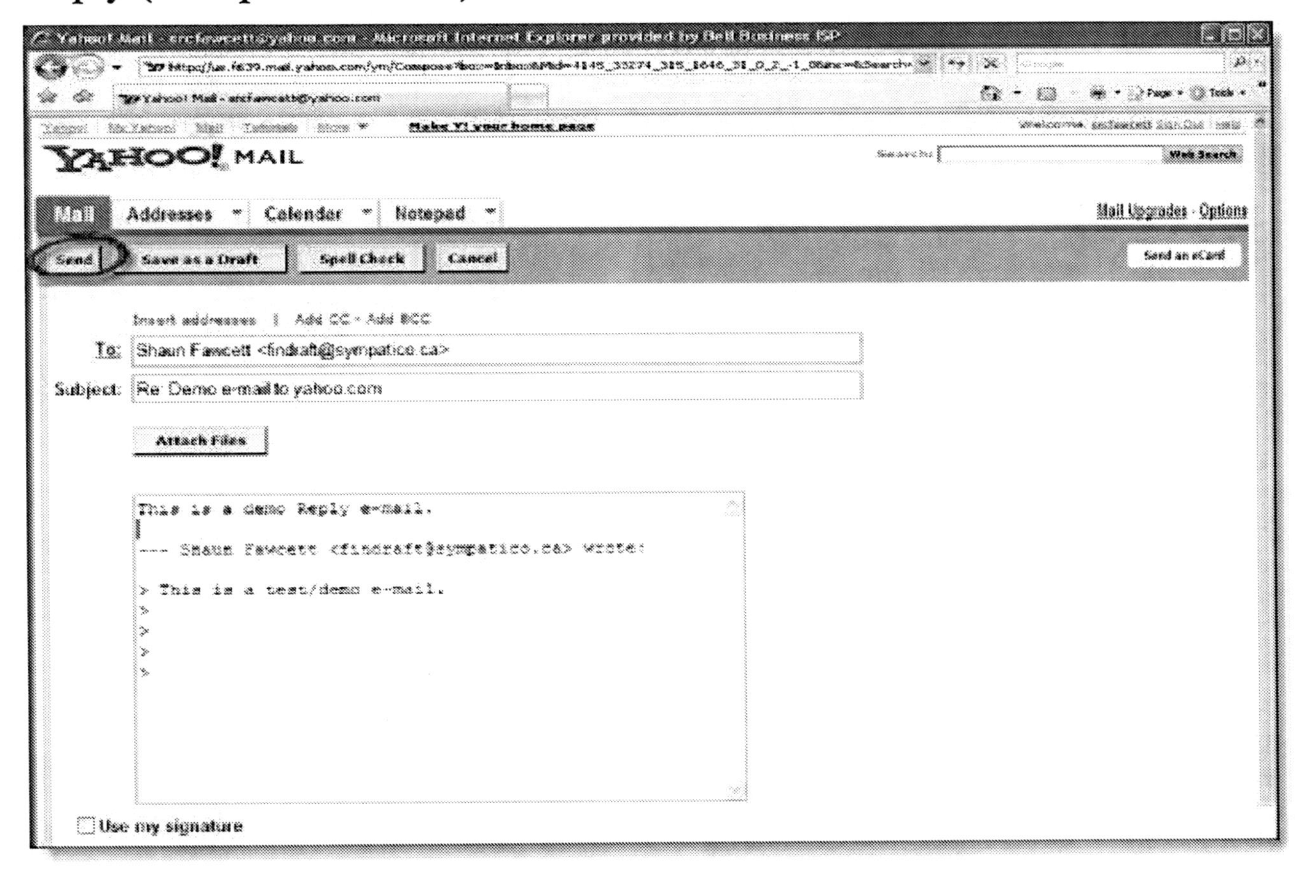

Note that Yahoo! Mail automatically inserts the text of the original e-mail to which you are replying into the bottom of your new e-mail.

Once you have added your Reply in the text window as per above, simply click on the Send button on the E-Mail Action Toolbar.

When you click on the Send Button you will be taken to a Send Confirmation Screen where you will then have the option to add the current addressee to your Address List. (If it's an address not already on the list). The Yahoo! Mail software will maintain this ongoing "list of Contacts" for you. Following is the "Add Address" screen.

Add Recipients To Address Book

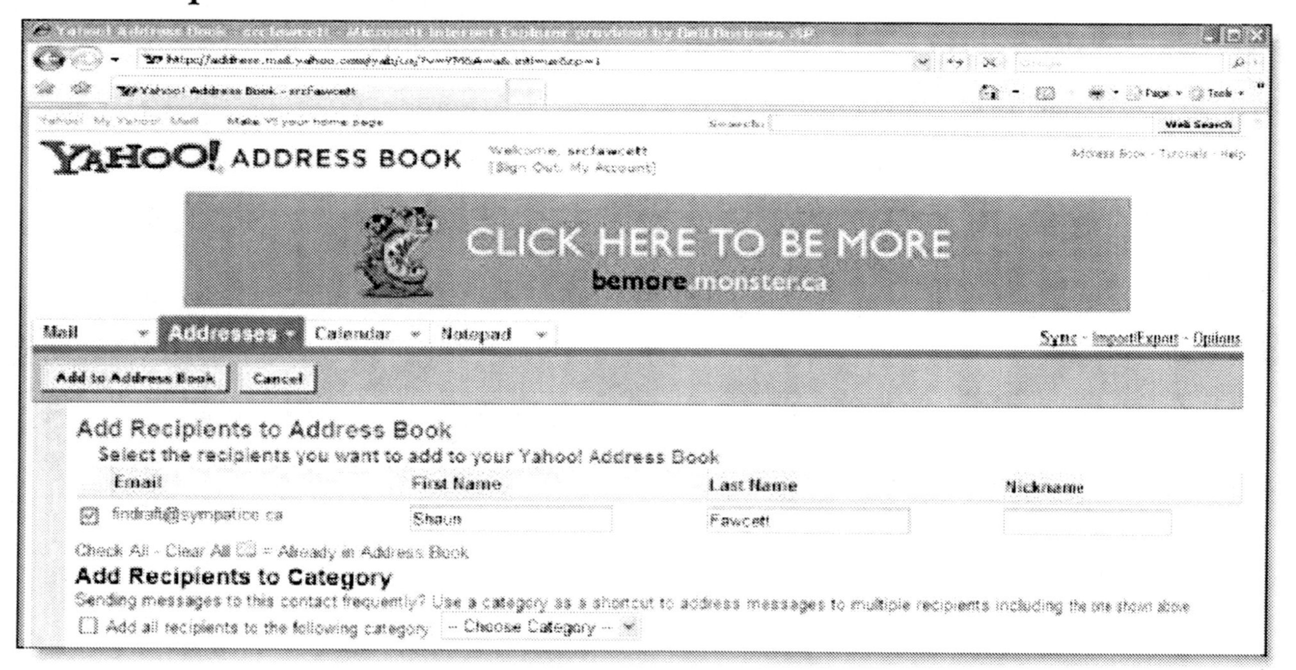

Sending Attachments In Yahoo! Mail

To add attachments to your e-mail click on the "Attach Files" button just below "Subject" on the "Compose E-Mail" screen shown on the previous page.

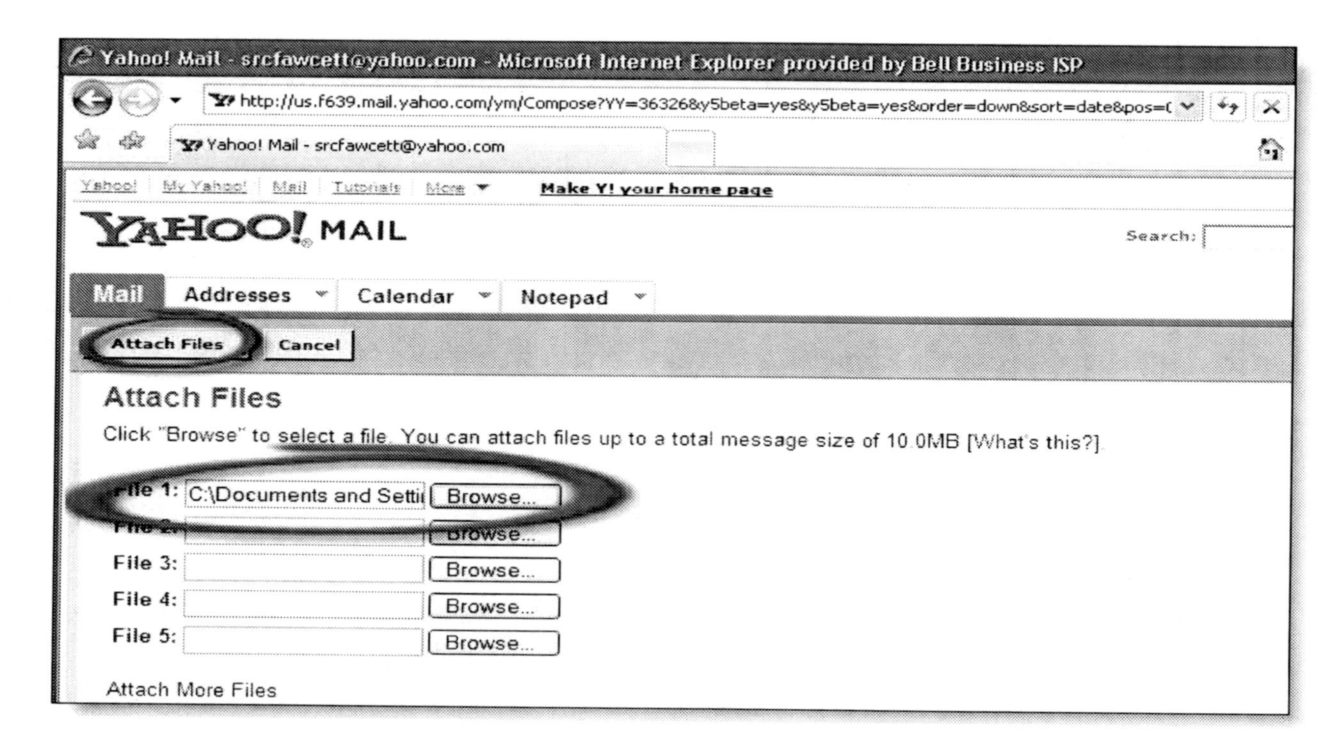

When the "Attach Files" screen opens as per above, you will have the option to browse through the files on your hard drive. Once you have browsed to the file you want to Attach, double click on it and it will be listed, as per "File 1" in the above screen shot.

When you have finished attaching all files that you wish to attach to the current e-mail you are composing, click on the "Attach Files" button as highlighted in the upper left corner of the above screen shot. That will reveal the following confirmation window.

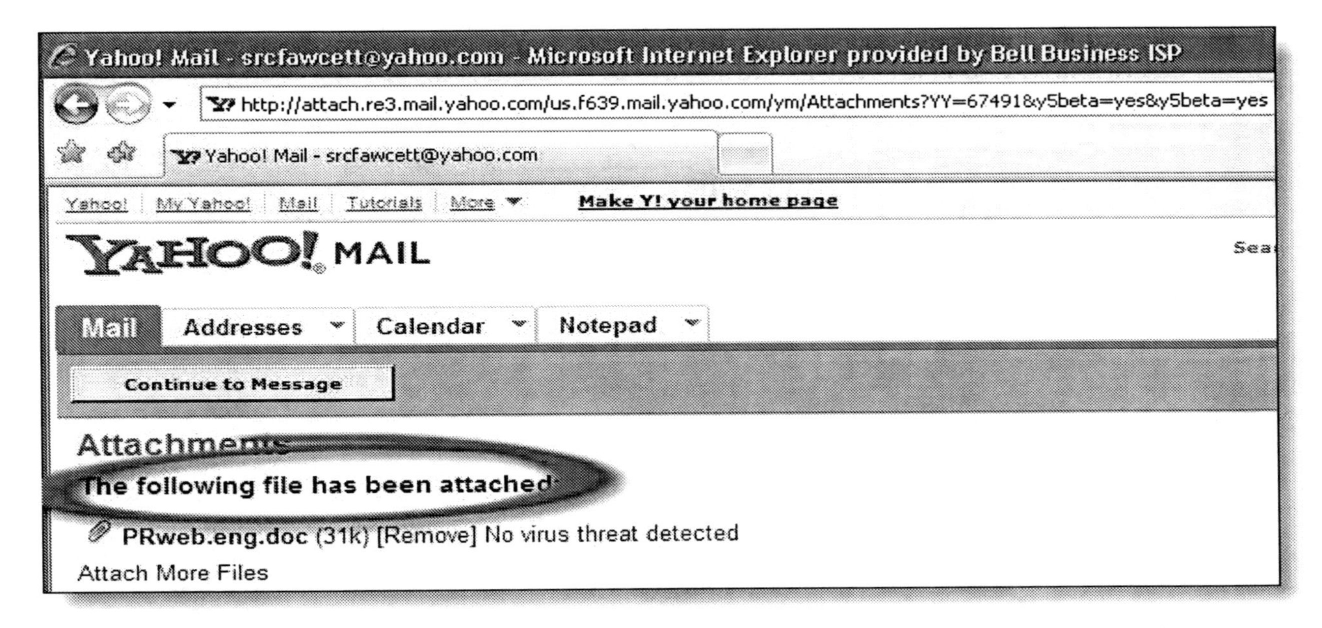

Clicking on "Continue to Message" button will display the message with attachment as shown below to the right of the arrow.

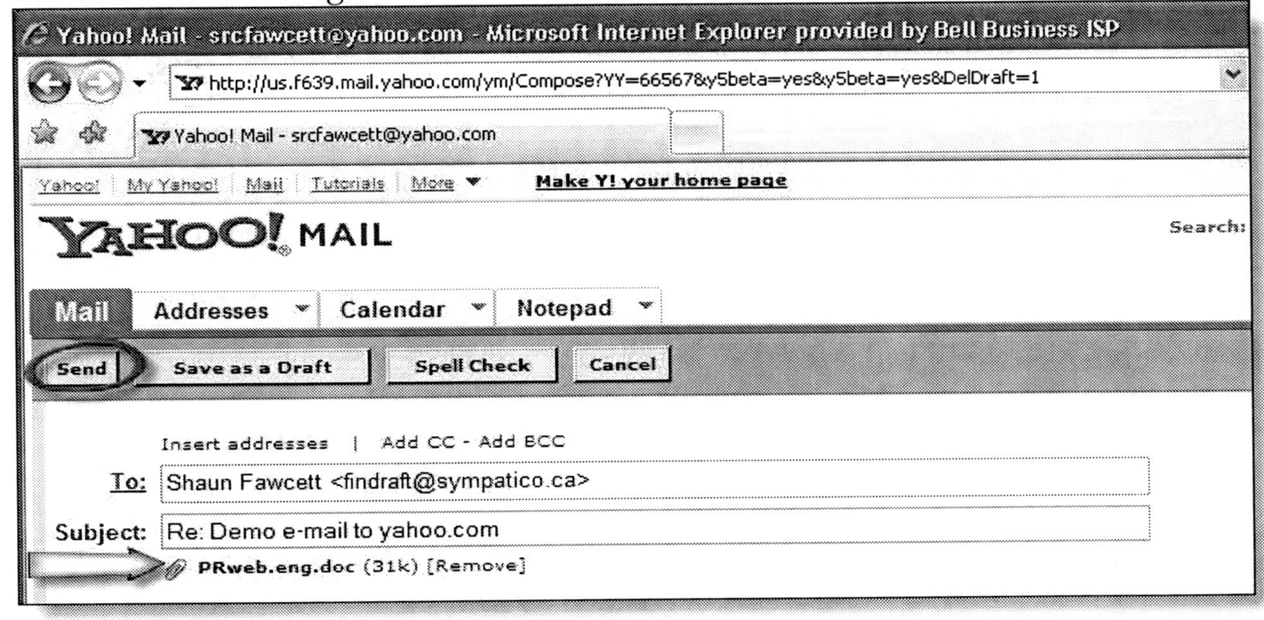

Sending An E-Mail In Yahoo! Mail

Once you have completed composing your e-mail and adding any attachments you can send it simply by clicking on the "Send" button on the Compose E-mail Screen. That will immediately open a "Reply Sent" window as shown below.

Reply Sent Confirmation

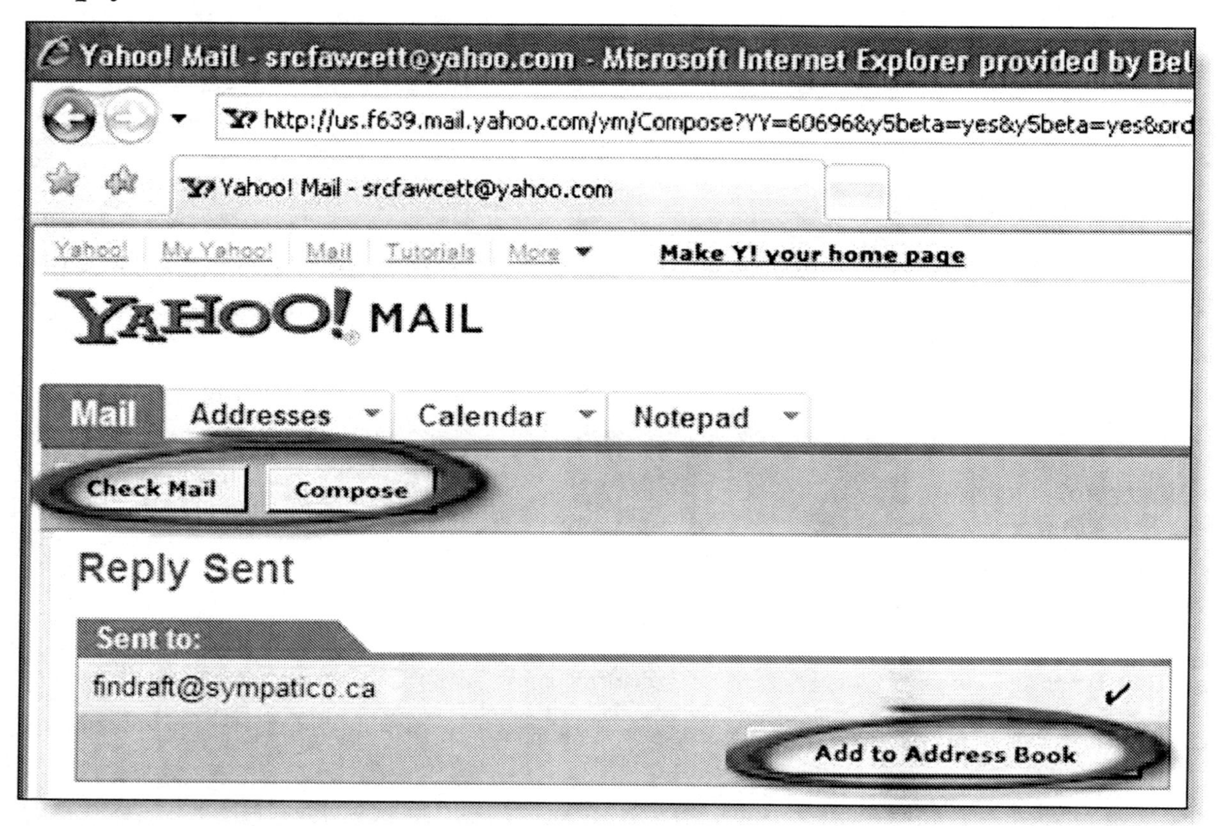

Once you are at this "Reply Sent" screen you have a choice of three actions as follows:

Add to Address Book

Click on this button to add the current addressee to your e-mail address list.

Check Mail

Clicking on this button will take you back to your main Inbox Screen.

Compose

Clicking on the "Compose Button" will open the Compose E-mail Screen.

Selecting E-Mail Options In Yahoo! Mail

To select various e-mail option settings in Yahoo! Mail, first click on the main "Mail" tab and then click on the "Options" button as highlighted on the screen below.

Mail Status Screen

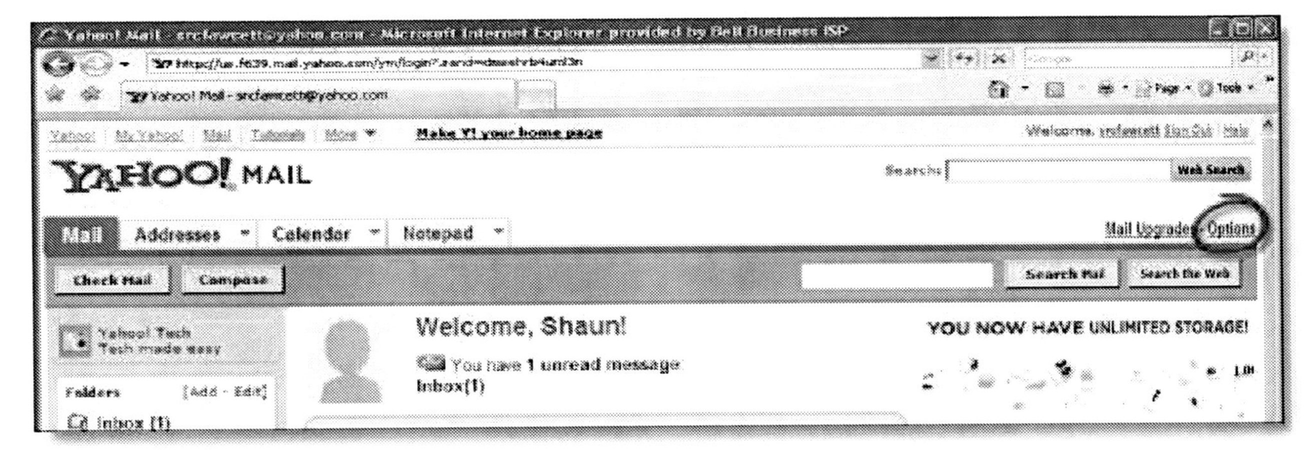

Clicking on the "Options" button will open the Mail Options screen as follows:

Yahoo! Mail Options

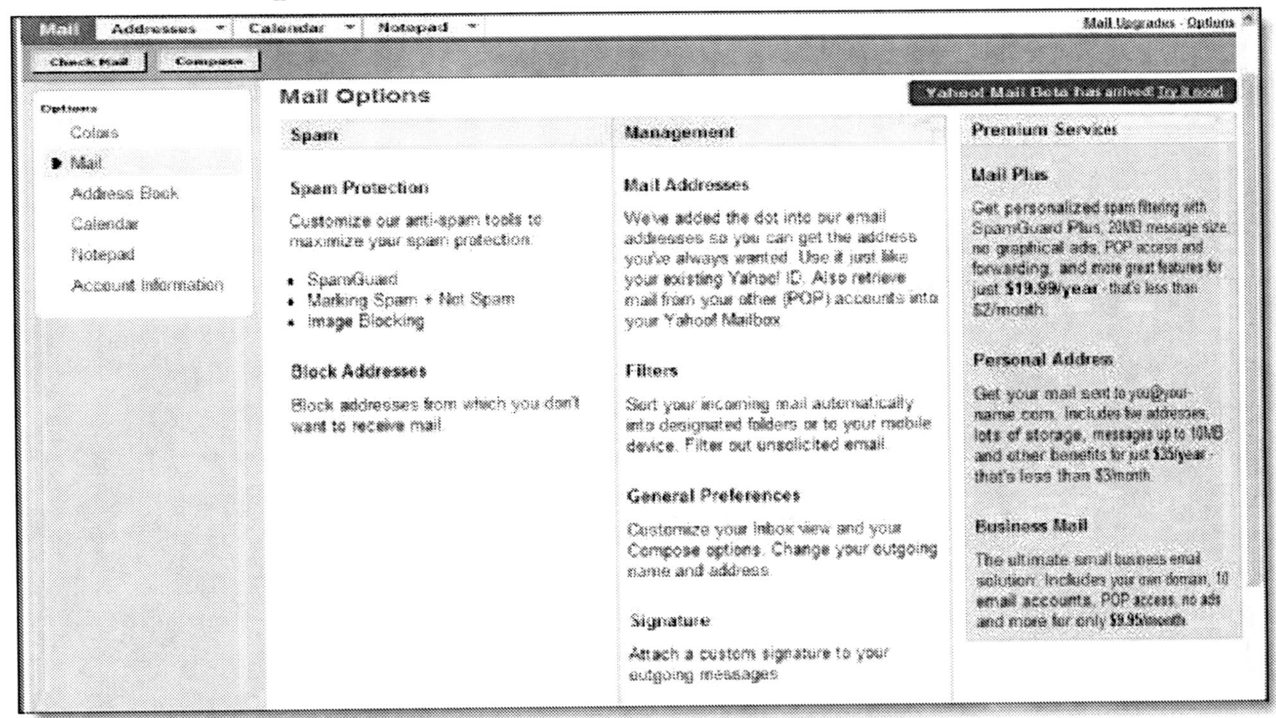

I will not go into the details of any of the options here. If you want to explore them, simply click on the appropriate heading and check it out. One point to note with Yahoo! Mail is that the options listed in the shaded column on the right are NOT free.

HOW TO SURF THE NET

Before I get into the details of exactly what's involved in surfing the Net there are some basic terms and definitions that you need to know in order to be fully effective.

Introduction To Web Surfing

If you have opened this book straight to this section, I strongly suggest that you take a few minutes right now to review the very first chapter titled *What You Need To Know First* (see page 9).

That section explains a number of key terms and definitions that you will need to know and understand to be able to browse the Web effectively. The two most important of those terms for you to understand are: Browser (see page 9) and Virtual Clipboard (see page 14).

I also suggest that you review the sections on *How To Copy and Paste* (see page 15) and *How To Cut and Paste* (see page 17) since it is likely that you will want to use these features often while surfing the Net.

Your Web Browser Program

Web Browsing - Definition

The term "browsing" is bandied about a lot, but what does it really mean?

It's simple actually. To "browse the Web" means to move from website to website to find specific information you are seeking, and/or to explore what new information you can find at the destination sites. Browsing is done via your "browser program", such as MS Internet Explorer or Mozilla Firefox. (see page 9).

In fact, to be able to browse the World Wide Web you need to have a browser program installed on the computer you are using.

How To Activate Your Browser Program

Once your computer is connected to the Internet, activate your browser program; if that doesn't already happen automatically at start-up. Most people have it set up so that their browser window is the one that opens up "on top" by default.

If not, you can open your browser by clicking on the icon that activates that program. For example, for personal preference reasons, I have my computer start-up set so that my browser program does NOT open automatically when I fire it up. When I want my browser I double-click on the appropriate icon on my Desktop, as per the following:

As I mentioned earlier, I use MS Internet Explorer as my main browser. Although from time-to-time I also open Mozilla Firefox and view certain websites with it; for technical reasons that I won't go into here. Normally, when you sign up with an ISP company, part of that procedure will involve the installation of a default browser program.

I also have quick access to either one of these browser programs by clicking on the icons located on my Windows Toolbar at the bottom of my Desktop screen. The Internet Explorer icon on the left and a Firefox icon on the right, as follows:

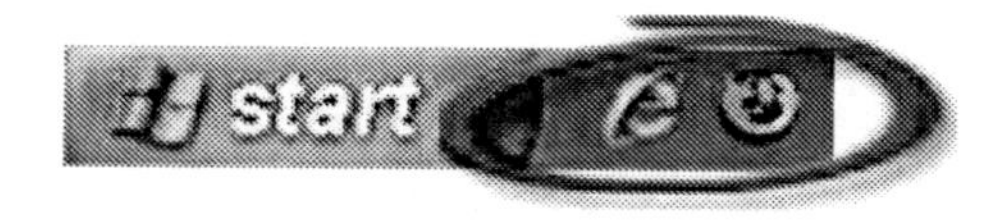

You might also have one of these icons set up on your toolbar since these shortcut icons are often added automatically when the browser program is first installed on your computer. In any case, it doesn't matter which icon you click to activate your browser program, as long as double-clicking it opens the browser that you want to use.

Since Internet Explorer is used by more than 85% of all users connected to the Web at this time, it is the browser that I focus on in this guide. If you are a beginner, I suggest that you stick with IE unless you have a good reason to do otherwise.

Your Browser Start-Up Window

When I double-click on one of my Internet Explorer icons it opens automatically to one of my websites which I have set as my browser home page (writinghelptools.com). Don't worry; you can change that default opening page to whatever YOU want. I'll show you how to do this a little bit later. (see page 95).

Below is the actual page that opens into my Internet Explorer browser when I click on one of the icons to open that program.

Internet Explorer Browser – Opening Screen

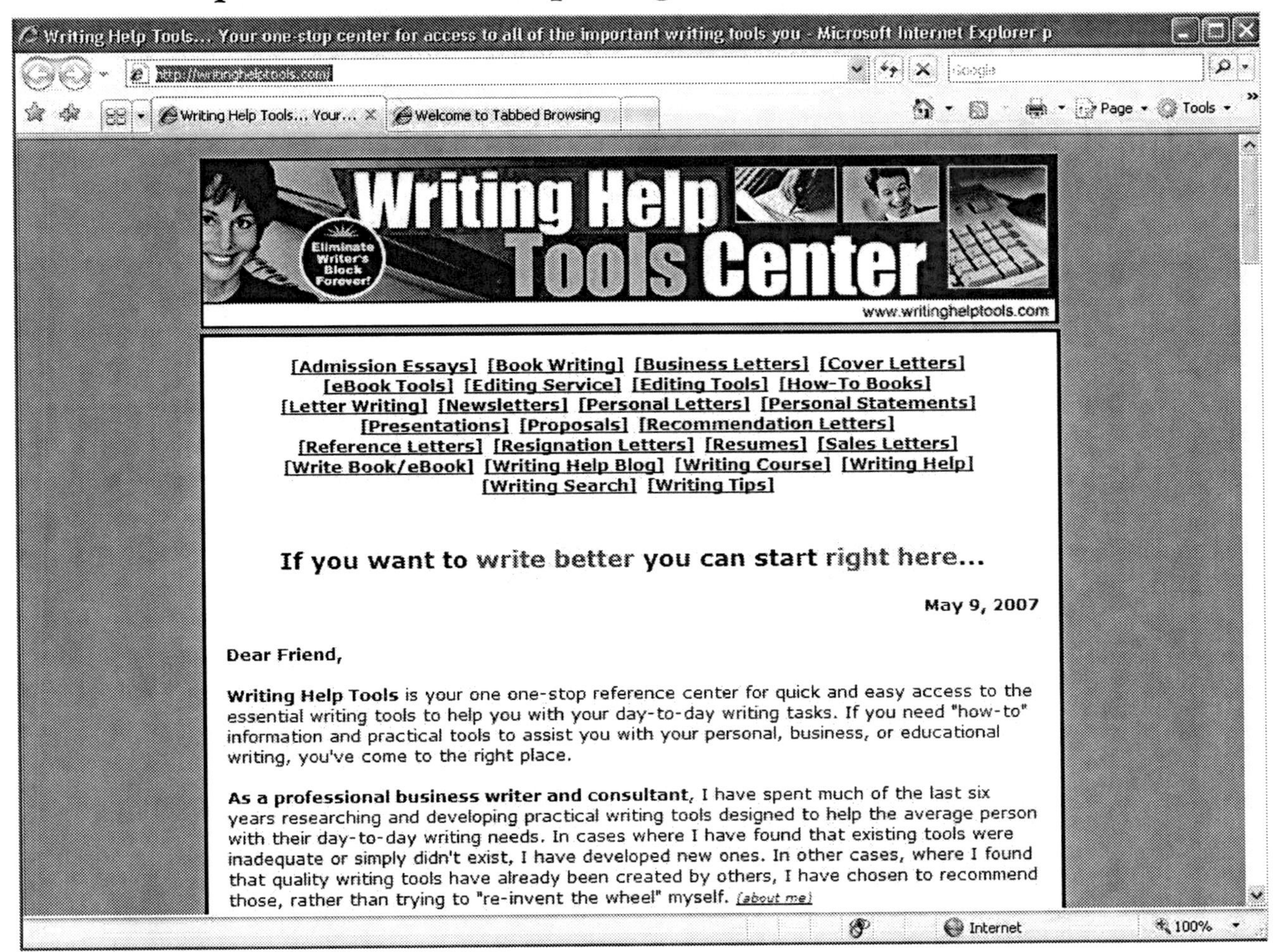

The content of the viewing area isn't really important at this point since that can be whatever you want it to be just by specifying (i.e. surfing to) another Web address.

The important issue here is what you can do with the toolbar panel at the top of the browser, something I will explain in more detail on the following pages.

So that you can see clearly that the browser program you use has very little impact on what you actually see, here's that same Web page as viewed in Mozilla Firefox.

Mozilla Firefox Browser – Opening Screen

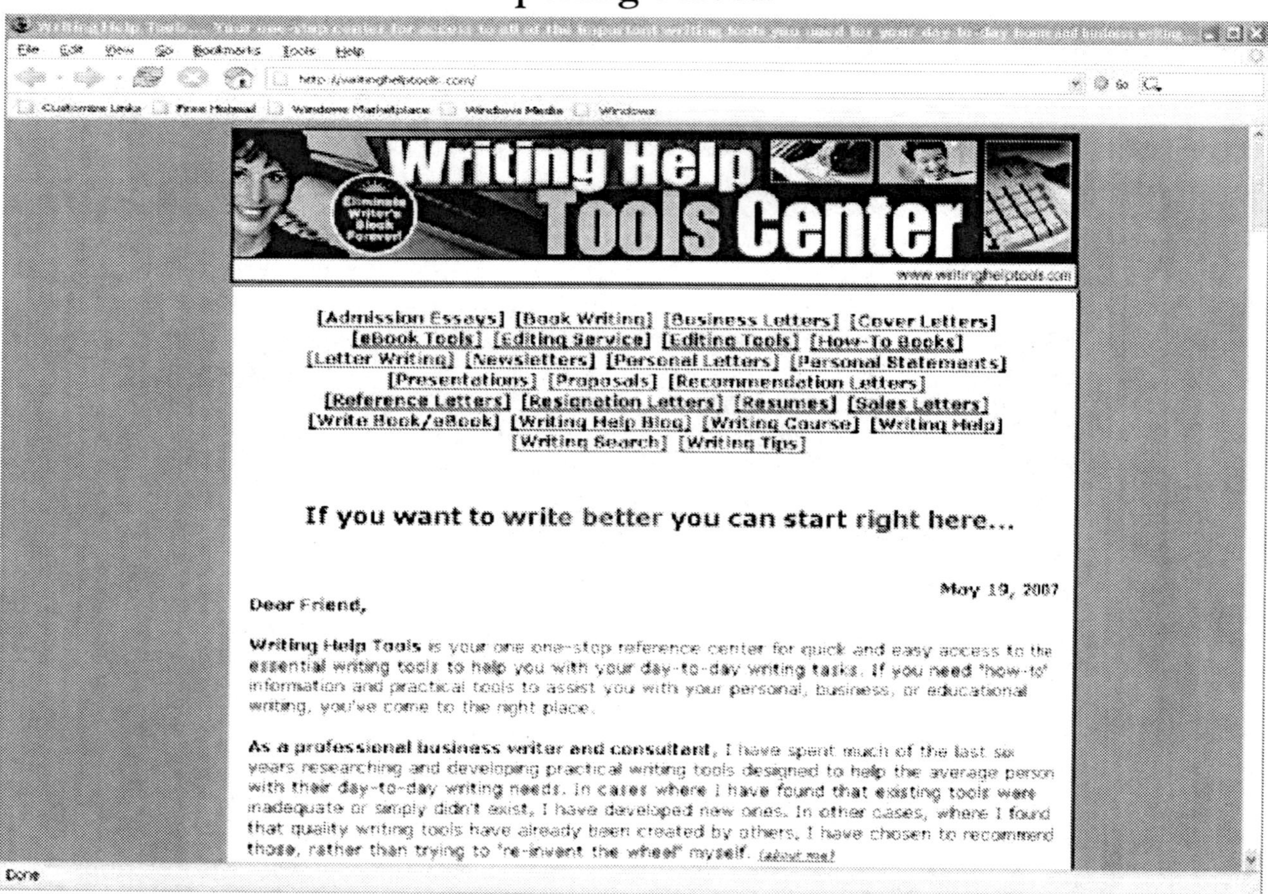

In fact, if you carefully compare this Firefox window with the previous Internet Explorer window the only differences you will see are minor deviations in some of the line thicknesses and colors; that's in addition to the different toolbars of course.

Browser Toolbar Functions

As discussed earlier, although the browser toolbar for each different web browser will look a bit different, they all offer essentially the same functionality. Below are the toolbars for the two most used browsers, Mozilla Firefox and Internet Explorer.

Browser Toolbar - Mozilla Firefox

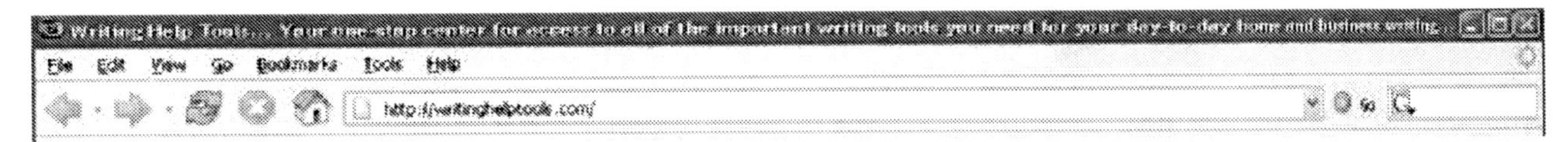

As explained in the Introduction, I am featuring Internet Explorer in this book because it is by far the most widely used Internet browser program. (i.e. over 85%).

Browser Toolbar - Internet Explorer 7.0

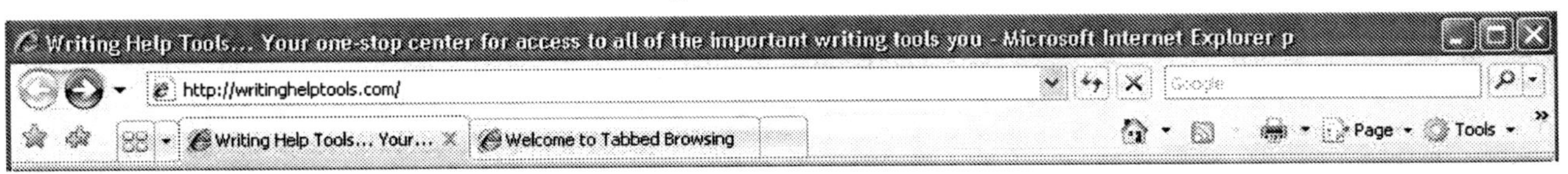

Following is a summary of the key basic functions available via the IE 7.0 toolbar.

Back/Forward Buttons

At the upper left of the toolbar are the Back button and Forward button. The left arrow takes you back to the page you just left. The right arrow takes you to the page you visited last, in the other direction.

Address/Location Field

This is the field that displays the actual Web address (or URL) of the website where your browser is currently positioned.

You can also edit that field any way you like. For example, if you want to go to another address just highlight and delete the current address and type the new address (i.e. URL) where you would like to go, and then hit your Enter Key.

Refresh/Stop Buttons

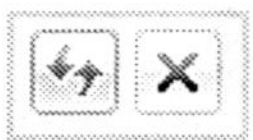

The Refresh button or Reload Button reloads the current website address into your browser to make sure you are viewing the latest version. The Stop Button can be clicked at any time to halt the current operation.

Search Window

This is the window where you can enter search terms to make direct searches of the Web or of the Web page you are currently on. Just enter the word or phrase into the window provided and click the magnifying glass, or just click the Enter Key.

Favorites Buttons

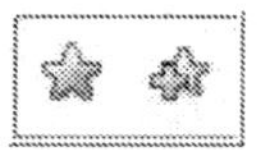

Clicking on the left-hand star will take you to your Favorites Center where you can view/manage previously saved favorite links. Clicking on the right-hand stars will let you add the current website to your Favorites List.

Window Tabs

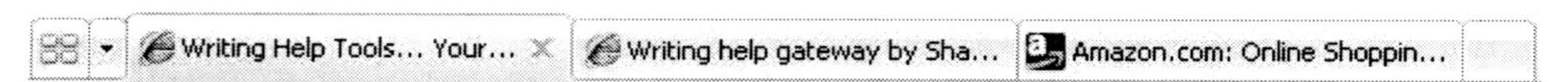

In Internet Explorer 7.0 and above (and in Firefox) you can open multiple active windows at one time and manage them from the Tabs Buttons, as shown above.

Home Page

Clicking on the Home Page Button will take your browser back to whatever URL you have set up as your default home page. Clicking on the dropdown menu arrow will let you change those home page settings.

Print Button

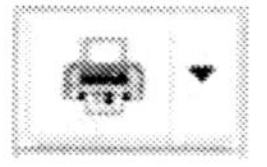

Clicking on the Print Button will print the page currently displayed in your active browser window. When you click on it, the standard Windows print dialogue box will open where you may change print settings as required.

Page Display Settings

New Window Ctrl+N
Cut Ctrl+X
Copy Ctrl+C
Paste Ctrl+V
Save As...
Send Page by E-mail...
Send Link by E-mail...
Edit
Zoom
Text Size
Encoding
View Source
Security Report
Web Page Privacy Policy...

Clicking on the Page dropdown menu arrow will reveal numerous actions that you can take on the page you are currently viewing in your browser's active window.

Since these options are mostly self-explanatory I am not going to cover them in detail here. Just activate the dropdown menu yourself and experiment with the various options as you wish.

Note that "Send Page by E-mail" and "Send Link by E-mail" will open a new Compose E-Mail window so that you can Compose and Send an e-mail. The only other of the above functions that I use occasionally are "Save As..." and "Text Size".

Tools Available

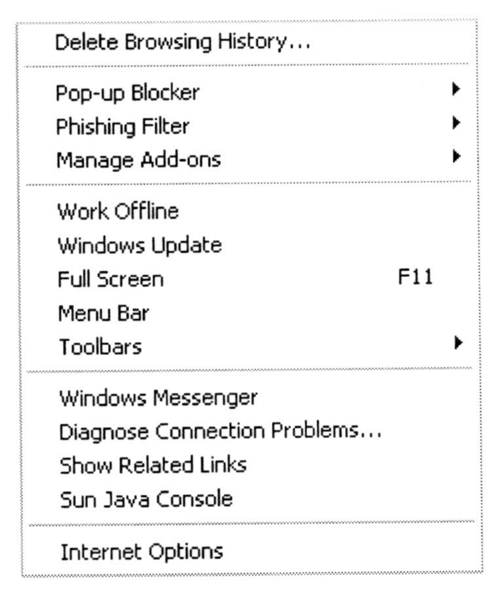

Clicking on the Tools dropdown menu reveals a variety of tools that are available to you from within your browser. Many of these are self-explanatory and you can check them out as you see fit.

The only Tools item that I am going to address in more detail a bit later on is the "Internet Options" item at the end of the list. (see page 99).

The only other of these functions that I use occasionally is "Toolbars". (see page 95).

Again, even though the above section deals specifically with the toolbar functions of Internet Explorer, you will find all of the same functions on the other major browsers.

Browser Options Settings

The **Internet Options** window in MS Internet Explorer is where you can set all of your preferences related to surfing the Net and viewing Web pages via your browser.

Similar to what I did with E-Mail Options earlier, I am only going to cover the options that I think will be of possible interest to the typical Internet beginner.

Accordingly, what I consider to be the most relevant Internet Options Tabs are as follows: **General**, **Security**, **Privacy**, and **Programs.** As I said, these are the four (4) tabs that are most useful and relevant for basic Internet surfing.

Feel free to check out any of the other Options if you wish.

There is a very important point to remember whenever you change or adjust the settings in ANY one of the Options tabs, as follows:

First; after you have made your changes, click on the **Apply** button on the bottom right corner of the tab.

Second; click on **OK** on the bottom left to save the new settings and close the tab.

Please Note: All of the settings applied in the Tabs that are shown on the following pages are as I have set them for my specific situation. You can change these to suit your own needs.

General Internet Options Tab

The **General** Options tab allows you to set your overall preferences for your browser.

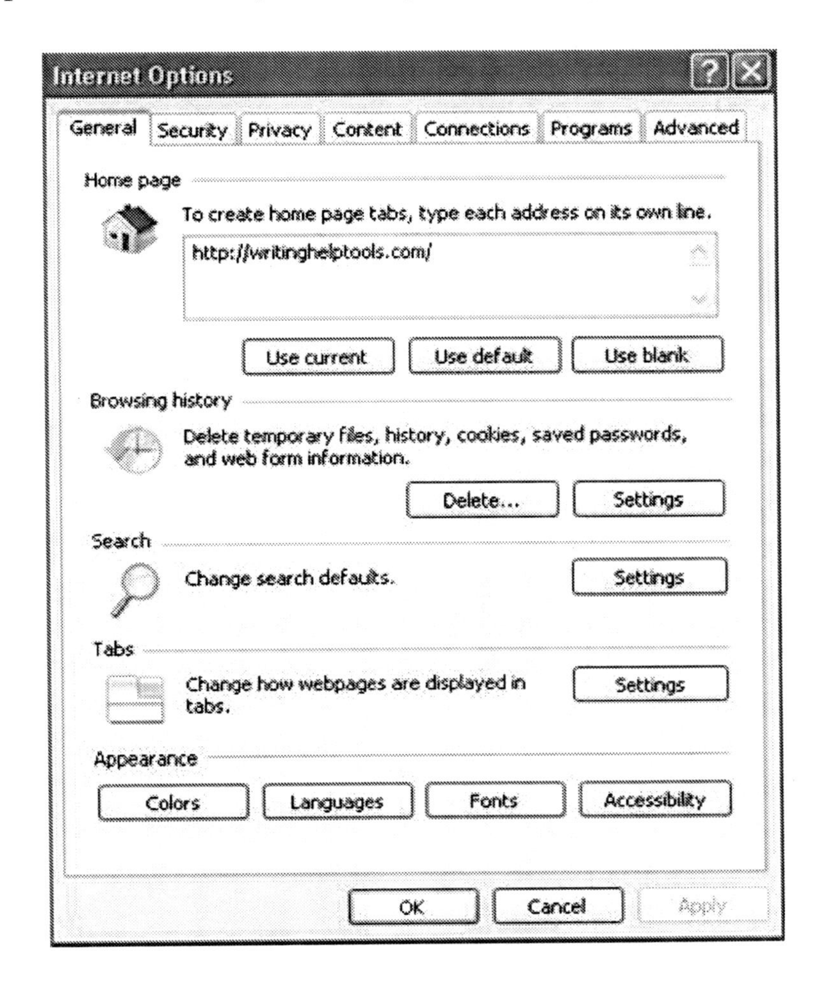

The main point here is that this is where you can change the URL address of the page that will open automatically when your browser program opens. As explained earlier, I have my home page set to one of my own websites "http://writinghelptools.com", as you can see above. You can set this to any URL that you wish.

The only other of the above settings that I have ever needed to use are the Colors and Fonts settings, under the Appearances heading, near the bottom of the tab..

For basic surfing I don't think you will ever need to be concerned with "Browsing History", "Search" or "Tabs" settings. Although, feel free to check them out.

Security Internet Options Tab

The **Security** Options tab allows you to adjust the security settings related to the websites that you access via your browser.

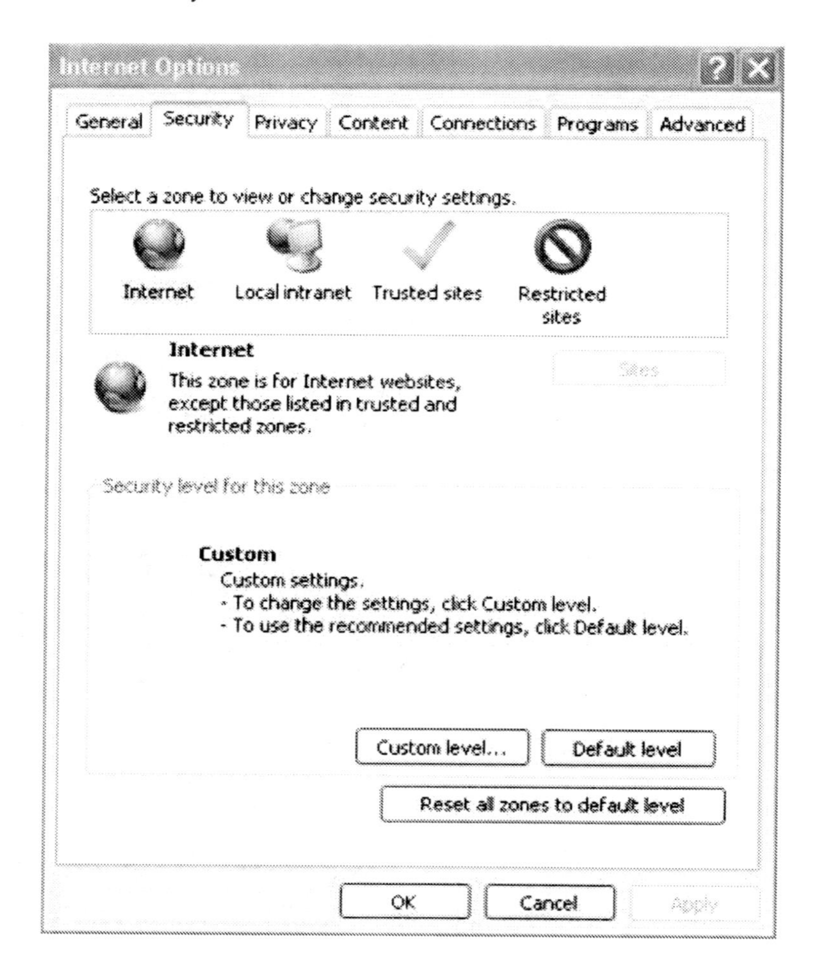

I'm showing you this tab just to let you know that it does exist and circumstances may come up when there is a good reason to adjust them. Among other things, this tab allows you to restrict browser access to certain websites, or to block specific websites.

However, unless you really know what you are doing I strongly suggest that you stick with the original default settings.

Take note that if you do make a change(s) to deal with a particular situation you can reset everything to the original default settings by clicking on the "Reset" buttons indicated at the bottom of each tab.

Privacy Internet Options Tab

The **Privacy** Options tab lets you control to what degree websites you access can write identification information (called "cookies") on to your computer's hard drive.

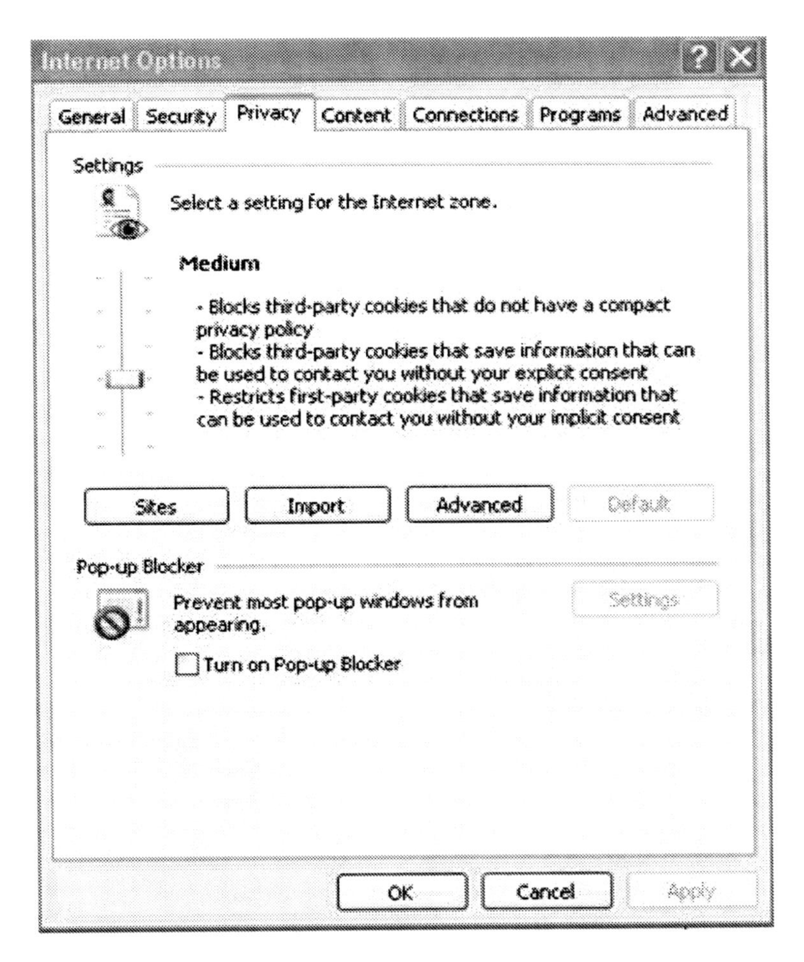

My Privacy settings are set to the Medium default level, which works well for me. If you make this setting too restrictive, every time you return to certain trusted sites to which you have given your identification info you will have to re-enter that info over again.

As you can see above, I have chosen to NOT "Turn on Pop-up Blocker" to block pop-up windows, as a personal preference. Since I sell my products online I learn from pop-ups. I like to see what they are offering and then I close them myself.

Again as with the Security Options, unless you really know what you are doing I strongly suggest that you stick with the original default settings.

Programs Options Tab

The **Program** Options tab gives you the ability to change the default programs that are automatically assigned for certain functions such as e-mail and Internet browsing.

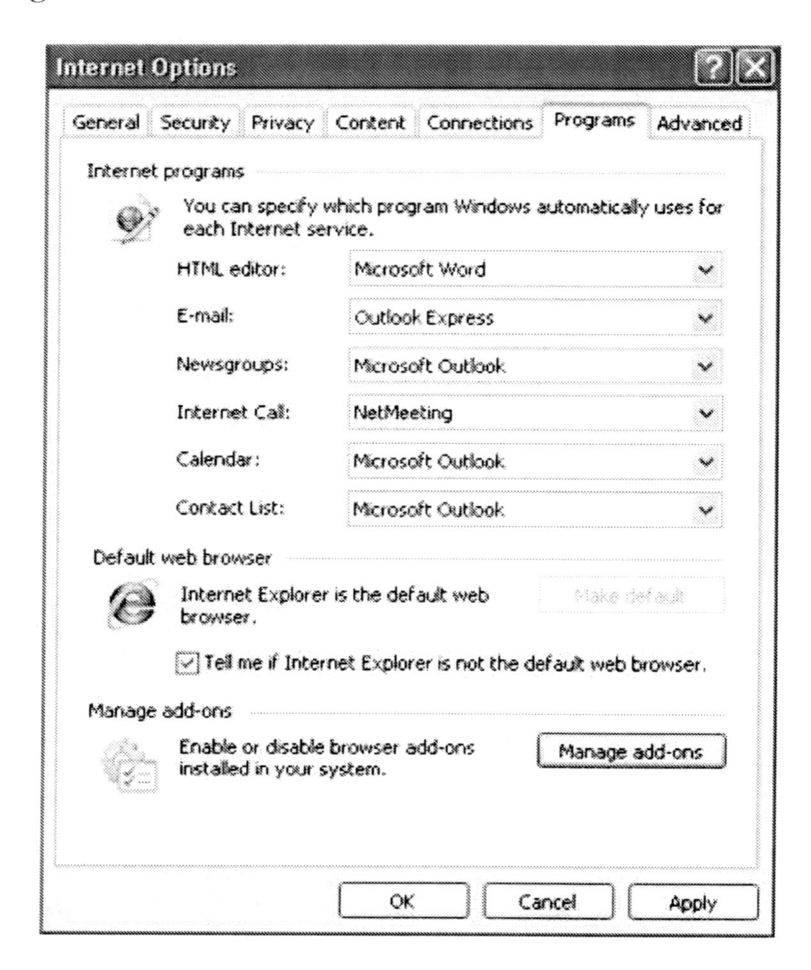

The only one of these settings that a beginner might want to change is the "Default web browser" setting.

Typically, you would do this in a case where you want to change browser programs from your current one to a new one that you have just installed. For example, say you decide you want to switch from Internet Explorer to the Mozilla Firefox browser; you would want to use this tab to set Firefox as your new default browser.

Although often, when you install new browser software the installation program will ask you about whether you want to change this setting, so you won't have to do it here.

Other Useful Browser Options

In addition to what you can do via the Internet Options tabs covered on the previous pages, there are a few other things that an Internet beginner could find helpful as well.

How To Select Browser Text Size

If you are having trouble reading what is on the Web page you are viewing, you can easily change the size of the text on that page. To do this in Internet Explorer 7.0 click on the Page icon on the toolbar and then select the Text Size item on the dropdown menu, as follows.

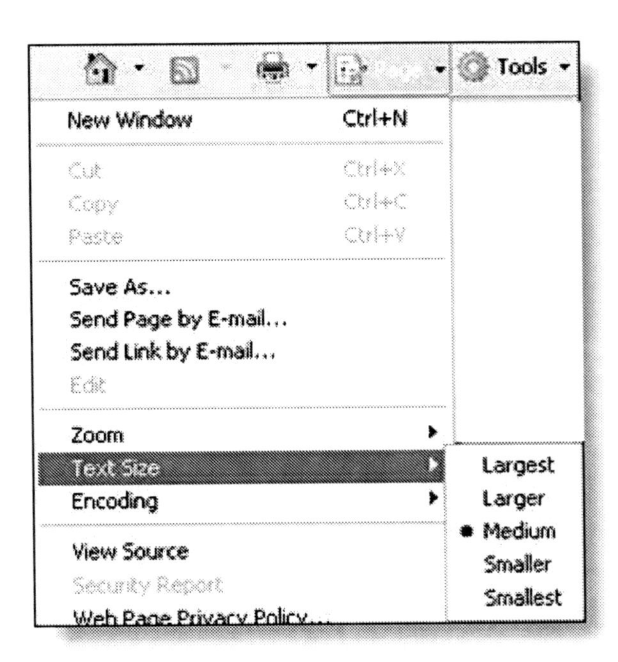

How To Add/Change Toolbars

You can also add other toolbars to your browser, in addition to the standard toolbar that comes with your browser. Typically, these are special add-on toolbars that some companies offer so that you can have one-click access to their products or services from your browser toolbar.

For example, Google offers a toolbar add-on that you can download and install as part of your browser toolbar. Various other companies offer these as well. **It is important to note that YOU MUST install a toolbar before it will be available to Select.**

How To Select Toolbars

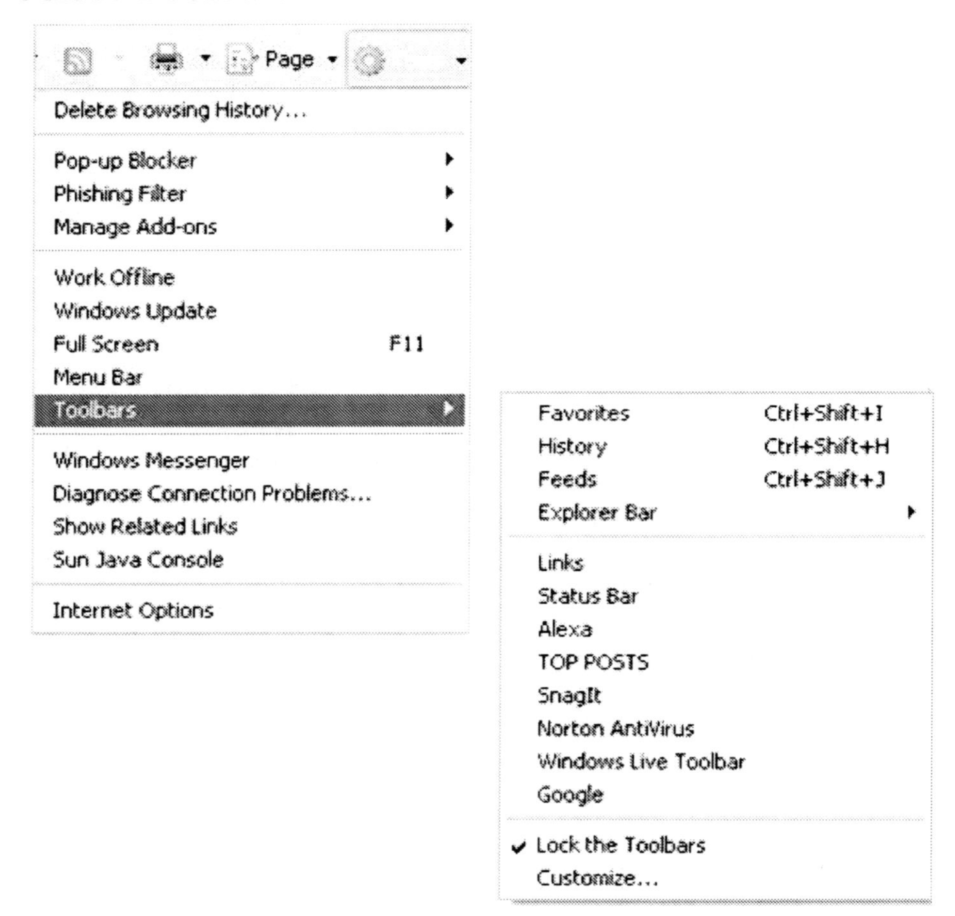

To add already installed toolbars to your browser toolbar, first click on the Tools Button on the main toolbar and then click on the Toolbars item on the menu. That will reveal a list of toolbars that are installed on your computer which are available to add to your main toolbar. Just click on the item on the list that you want to add and a checkmark will appear beside it to show that it is enabled. The next time you look at your toolbar it will include the add-on(s) toolbar that you just selected.

For example, as you can see from the list above, the Google toolbar is available for me to add to my browser toolbar. What that means is that at some point in time I have deliberately chosen to install the Google toolbar on my computer. To do that, I went to the following URL and downloaded and installed that toolbar on my computer.
http://toolbar.google.com/T4/

Again, as explained above, to add that Google toolbar to your main browser toolbar just click on that item on the list of available toolbars (in this case "Google"), and a checkmark will appear beside it to show that it is enabled. Then, the next time you look at your main toolbar the Google toolbar will be integrated into it.

To make this absolutely clear, I have provided "before and after" screenshots below. The first one shows my basic Internet Explorer toolbar without the Google toolbar enabled. The second shows it with the Google toolbar enabled.

Main Browser Toolbar – No Add-Ons

Main Browser Toolbar – Google Toolbar Enabled

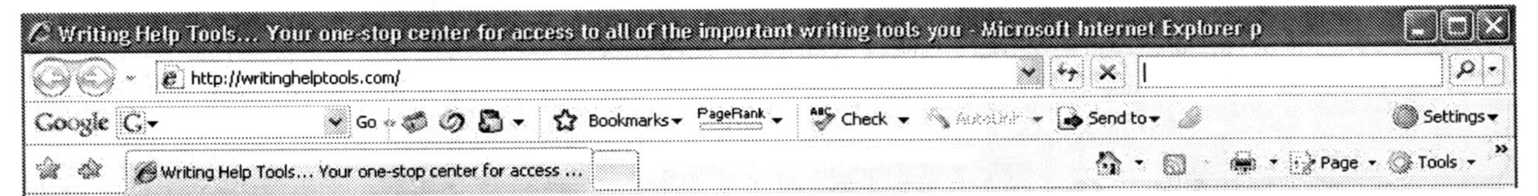

Important Note: Almost all add-on toolbars are first designed to work on the most popular browser program, Internet Explorer. I have found that a number of toolbars that I like to use are only available for IE and are not yet available to install in Mozilla Firefox. So, be sure to check this out before you decide on the combination of browser and add-on toolbars that you want to use.

Don't worry too much about add-on toolbars if you find them confusing. You can get around the Internet quite nicely without any add-ons installed. In other words, these toolbar add-ons are completely optional.

What You Need To Know Before Browsing

Just before you start browsing the net there are a couple of things you should know that will simplify the experience for you. First, it will be helpful for you to understand the basics of Internet addresses (URLs). Second, a familiarization with the primary Search Engines will also be useful.

How Internet Addresses (URLs) Work

There is a unique address for each page of information on the World Wide Web. That address is known as a Unique Resource Locator, usually referred to as a URL.

All URLs begin with the character string "www" which, if you'll forgive me for stating the obvious, stands for World Wide Web.

In the early days of the Internet you would have to enter into your browser address/location field the entire URL including the "www" prefixed by the character string "http://". So, for example, up until a couple of years ago, to get to my main writing help tools website you would have to enter the entire phrase: http://www.writinghelptools.com

Now, entering that entire URL is no longer necessary. To get to that exact same website all you have to enter into most browsers is "writinghelptools.com". Browsers have gotten smarter over the years and now only require the truly unique part of a URL.

The majority of URLs that you will encounter have a "**.com**" suffix which loosely means that it is a commercial website, as opposed to government or not-for profit organizations. There are two other URL suffixes that you will often see, as follows:

The URL suffix "**.org**" normally means non-profit organization. For example the URL of the United Nations is www.un.org. International Red Cross is: http://www.ifrc.org

The other URL suffixes that you will often see are two character country codes such as "**.us**" for the USA, "**.ca**" for Canada, "**.in**" for India, "**.uk**" for United Kingdom, etc.

Don't panic! You don't have to know anything about how these country codes work; and which one stands for which country. This was just to give you a general idea of some of the more common URL endings/suffixes that you will see.

There are usually different levels of URLs at most websites, so as to differentiate the various unique pages of information on the site. For example, my main writing help website has more than 200 unique pages of writing help content.

So, using that writing help info site as an example, here are how the URLs work:

Main Website home/index page:	www.writinghelp-central.com
Letter Writing entry page:	www.writinghelp-central.com/letter-writing.html
Resume Writing Entry page	www.writinghelp-central.com/resume-writing.html
Sample Letters entry page	www.writinghelp-central.com/sample-letters.html
Writing Articles entry page	www.writinghelp-central.com/articles.html

As you can see, each URL is unique with a name that relates to the specific content on that page. As I stated above, that particular website has more than 200 different URLs. Many websites have thousands of unique pages, each with a unique URL.

But don't worry; you won't have to memorize any long URL names! If a website is well designed, all you will have to do is go to the main page – usually known as the home page or index page. From there, you should be able to navigate to the information (i.e. webpages) that you want to see via the clickable links provided.

Important Note: Whenever you are at a webpage that interests you and you want to save the unique URL for possible future reference, just click on the "Favorites Button" on your browser's main toolbar. Using that function you can save that URL in clickable form for later one click access. (See page 95).

About Search Engines

Search Engines (SEs) are powerful computer programs that are constantly scanning the World Wide Web for information about new and updated websites and webpages that they find online, and then adding that info to their internal databases. You can then use one or more of these search engines to find sites and pages relating to your specific topics of interest. (That's the simple definition of course).

Essentially, search engines allow one to scrutinize the entire contents of the World Wide Web in seconds, based on how it existed at one specific point in time. Most of the main SE databases are updated on a daily basis, so it is quite possible that new information for the same search criteria will appear from one day to the next.

Once you start to search the Web for information of specific interest to you is when you will truly begin to comprehend the power of the Internet. With just a few clicks of the mouse you can search databases stored on literally hundreds of thousands of computers located all over the world. In a matter of seconds you can travel electronically all over the globe. My personal experience has shown that doing research on the World Wide Web can be both exciting and rewarding due to its sheer power in terms of depth, breadth, and immediacy of information available.

Getting connected to the Internet is one thing; knowing where you want to go is a whole other issue. As explained earlier, the Internet consists of millions of computers linking many millions of people. It also consists of millions of websites with millions of webpages, containing billions of pieces of information, any one of which you may be interested in. In early 2007 it was estimated by experts that there were more than 110 million unique websites online at that time.

Nevertheless, in spite of this massive volume of information, there is no single comprehensive central Internet directory listing all possible sites. And because of the decentralized nature of the Internet, there will never be ONE such authoritative source of all information. This is why Search Engines were invented as a tool to help you navigate the World Wide Web to find the information that you want.

The Big Three SEs

Fortunately, when it comes to search engines things have gotten significantly simpler over the years. Just a few years ago there were more than a dozen "important" search engines that you would have to be aware of and use individually if you wanted to make sure you had thoroughly researched a subject online.

Now there are only three (3) significant search engines that the average person needs to be aware of:

www.google.com (70%)

www.yahoo.com (20%)

www.msn.com (10%)

Those percentage figures in brackets are the estimated portion of total online searches estimated to be handled by each of these SEs when I wrote this.

Because google.com is the dominant search engine I rely upon it as my search engine of first choice. Not only does google.com handle the most searches but it is considered industry-wide to be the "best" SE in terms of total coverage and quality of results returned when a search is conducted. So, for day-to-day web searches I tend to use google.com.

Nevertheless, when I am working on a project for which it is important that I consider ALL possibilities I also conduct my searches at msn.com and yahoo.com. Once I have researched something at all three of these sites I am pretty confident that nothing important would have slipped through the cracks.

The only other search engine that sends any level of traffic to my writing help websites is www.ask.com; so you might want to try that one as well for some of your searches.

How To Surf With Your Web Browser

Once you have your browser set up the way you like it and you are familiar with how web addresses and search engines work, as described in the previous section, you are ready to start some serious Web browsing.

How To Enter A Search Term

These days you shouldn't need to go beyond your browser's toolbar to enter a search phrase into a major search engine. For example, the standard toolbar for the Internet Explorer 7.0 browser allows me to enter a search term straight into google.com.

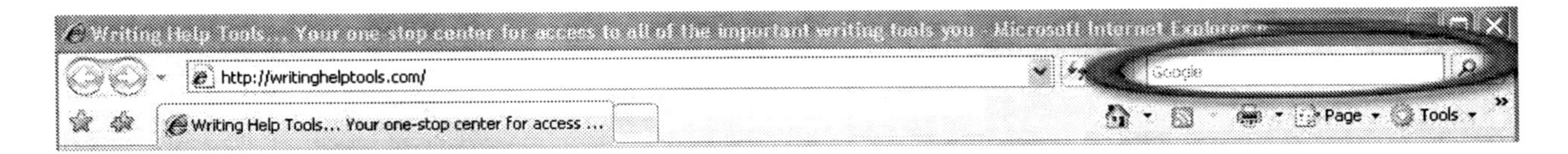

As you can see, that search box on the right actually displays "Google" in it when it is not in use. To enter a search term, just enter the term directly into that search box:

Sample Google Search – Using MS Internet Explorer Browser

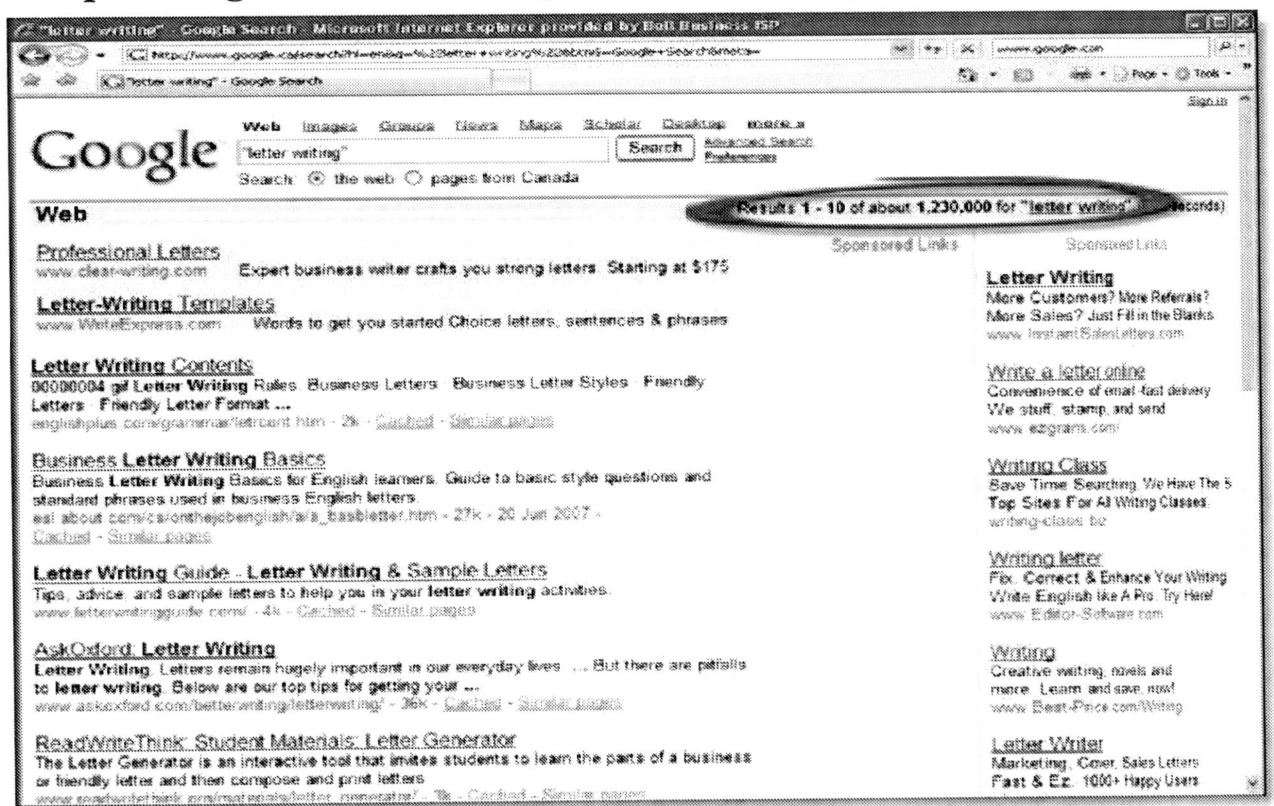

The results for that search term (i.e. "letter writing") will be displayed directly in your active browser window, just as shown above. Just click on the hyperlinks of interest.

Sample Google Search – Using Mozilla Firefox Browser

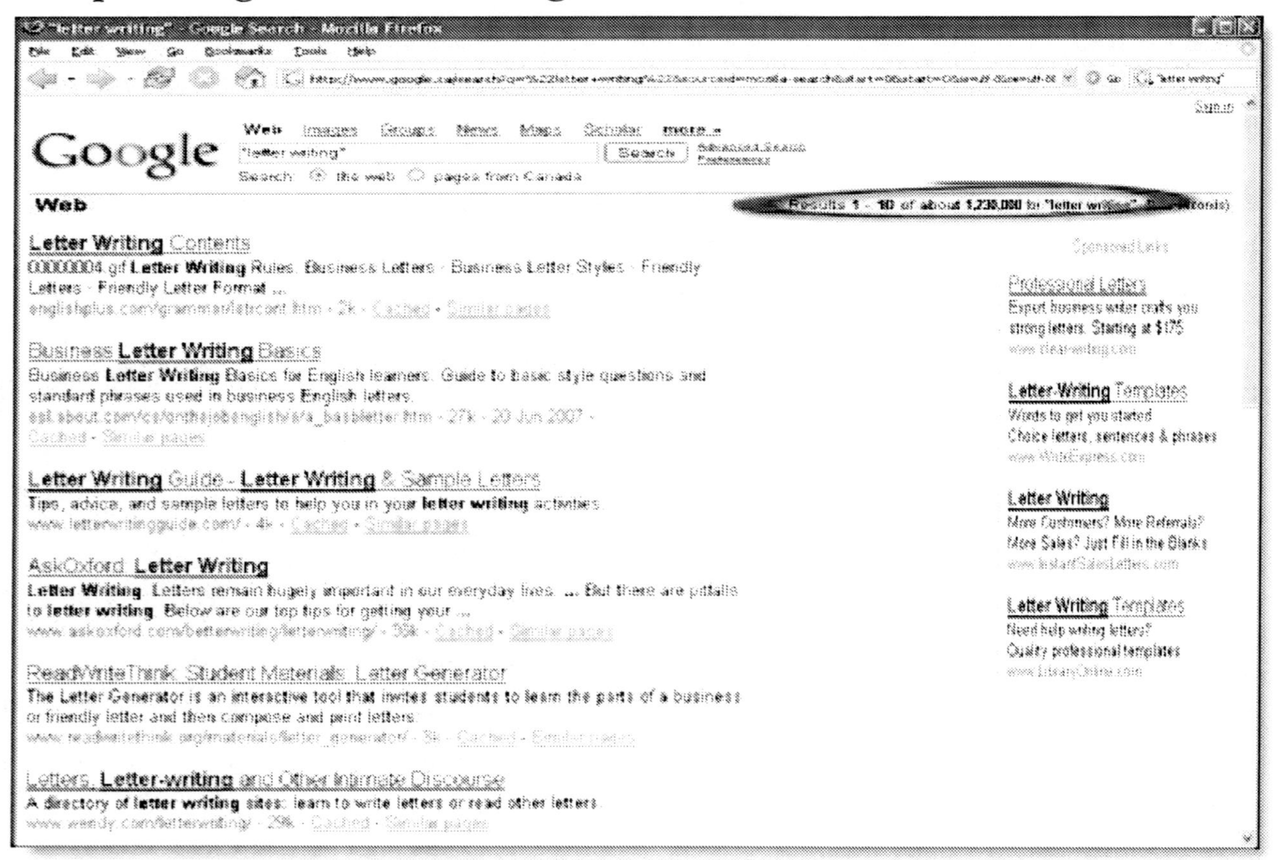

Notice that when you compare both browser results above (i.e. MS-IExplorer and Moz-Firefox), they are almost exactly the same. The only noticeable difference being the two sponsored ads listed at the top of the Internet Explorer results, while these were not displayed in the Firefox results.

You can also conduct searches from the home page of the search engines.

On the following page are screen shots of the search pages for the three main search engines. If you look above the "Search Term Entry Box" at each one of these you will see that there are various advanced search options available. For example, you can select ONLY Images, or ONLY News, to be included in your results. Other criteria such as Videos, Maps, Shopping, etc. are also available, depending on the SE you use.

The www.google.com main search box looks like the following:

The www.yahoo.com main search box looks like the following:

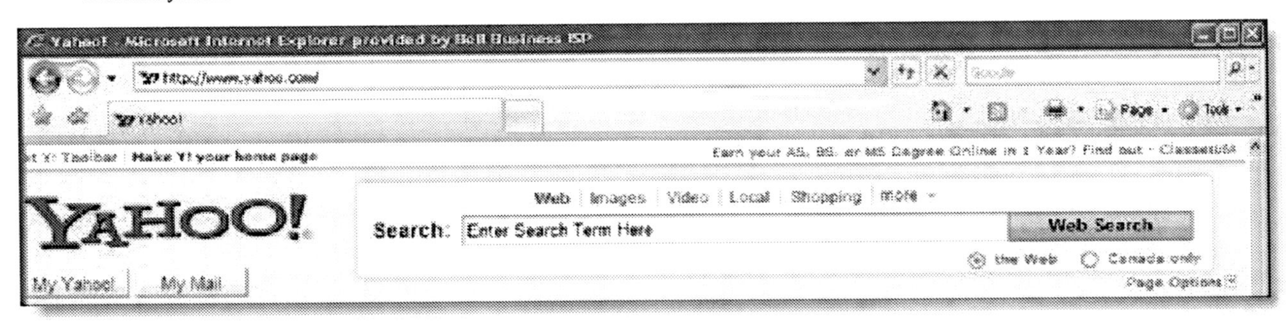

The www.msn.com main search box looks like the following

You will notice above that both google and yahoo offer me the option to select results from Canadian based pages only, apparently because I am based in Canada.

Frankly, I don't fully understand why they do this since the vast majority of my info searches involve the entire World Wide Web; NOT just Canadian pages. In fact, for someone like me who does business worldwide, this is a contradiction in terms.

Searches – Specific Content Options

As shown in the previous section, whenever you conduct a search via a standard search engine the default search mode is a "Web" search of online text-based content. So, in the sample searches done in the previous section, the search results returned were for text-based documents on the Web (As opposed to Images, Videos, Groups, etc.).

As is also pointed out in the previous section, in addition to text-based content, the major search engines offer a variety of other "specific-content" search types, such as: images, news, maps, video, and more; depending on which SE you use, as follows:

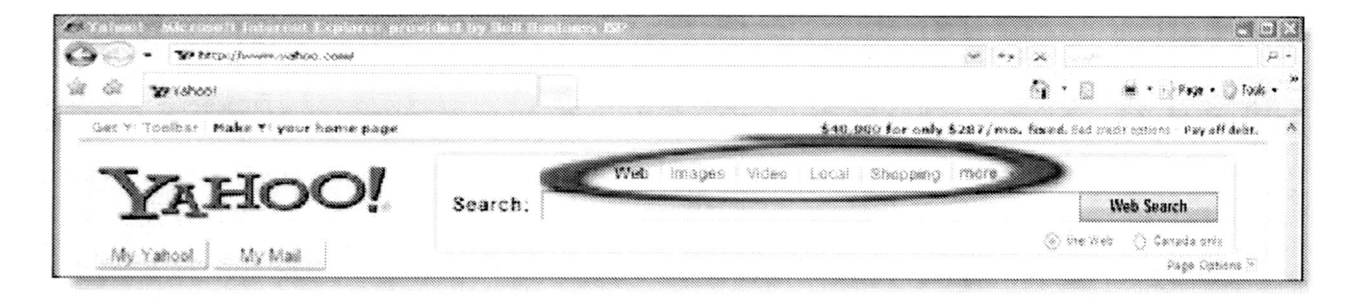

As shown above, to see these specific-content search options you must go to each SE's main page and view the list above the search box.

Sample Searches – "The Web"

For demonstration purposes I am going to use the search term "wild flowers" in the following search examples. There is no particular reason why I chose this particular phrase. It could have been anything.

On the following couple of pages are screen shots of search results for exactly the same search phrase using each of the top three SEs; google.com, yahoo.com and msn.com The main purpose of this is to show you how results are listed in each SE, as well as how the results differ between SEs, even for exactly the same phrase.

Sample Search – "Web" – Google

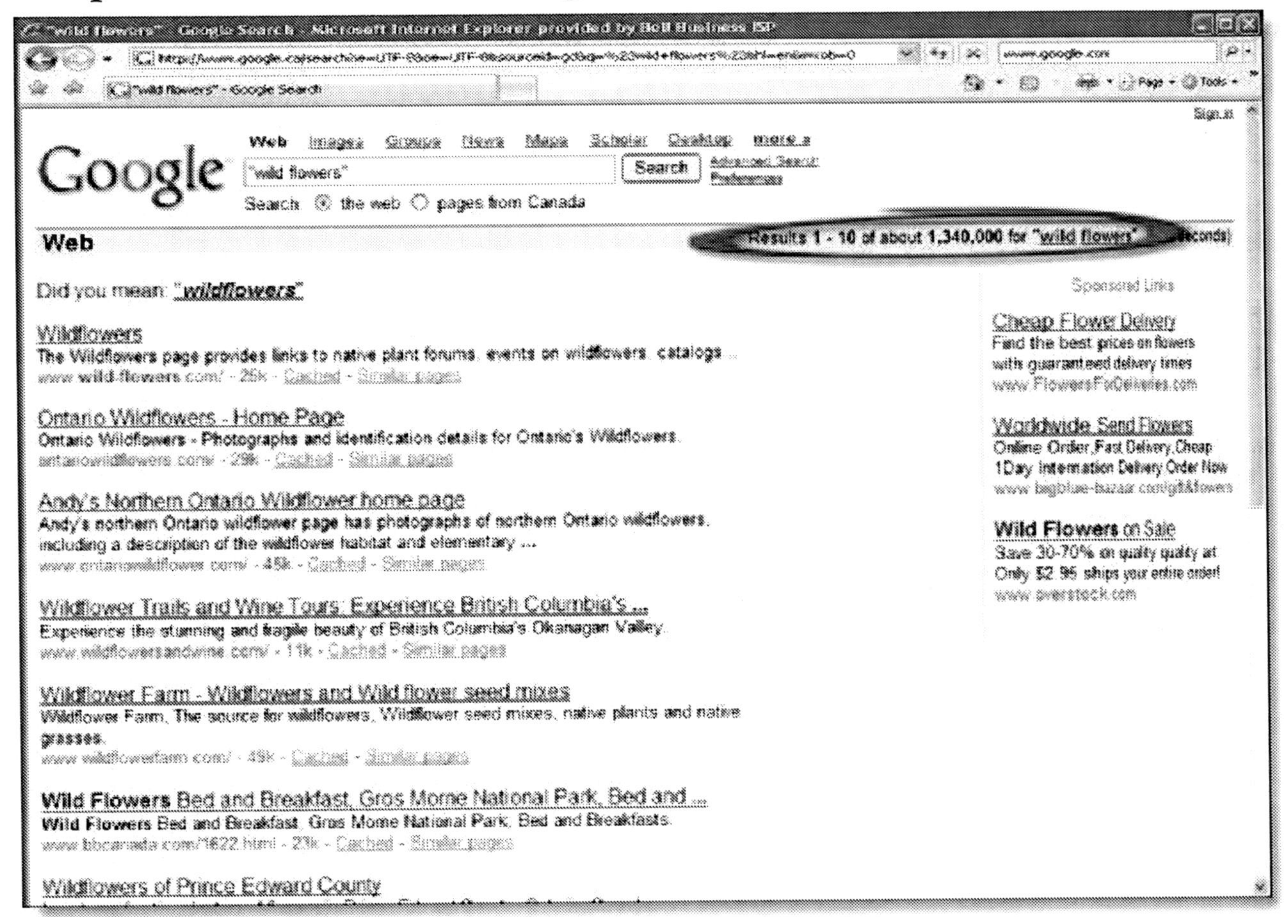

Notice from the highlighted Results message above that Google found more than 1.3 million pages online with specific reference to "wild flowers". However, as noted elsewhere, as you scroll down through the first few pages, the quality and relevancy of those results will quickly diminish.

Sample Search – "Web" – Yahoo!

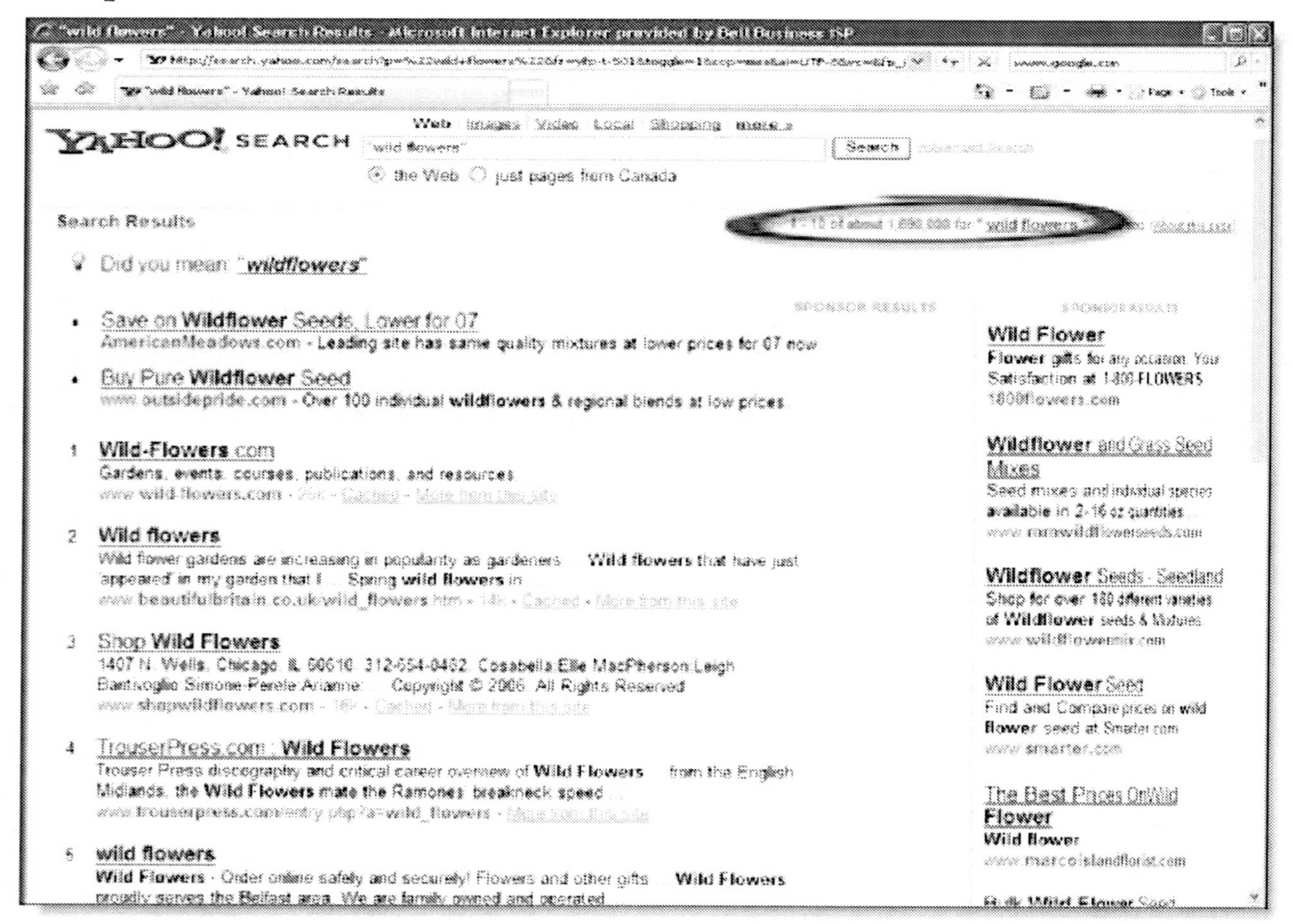

Note that the results listed down the right-hand side of the above page are paid advertisements. The generic ranked results are listed on the left side. However, as you can see, the first two (shaded) listings on the left are ALSO paid "Sponsor Results"..

As you can see from the Search Results line highlighted in the above screen shot, Yahoo found more than 1.6 million results for the phrase "wild flowers". However, as noted in the previous section, when you scroll down through the results you will see that they are becoming increasingly vague and less relevant by the fourth or fifth page.

Another point to note here is how these results produced by Yahoo! differ significantly from those returned by Google on the previous page. These significant differences in number of results found and relative ranking of results clearly illustrate how search engine results will vary among SEs for exactly the same search term. This is a direct function of their different proprietary search algorithms (formulas).

Sample Search – "Web" – MSN

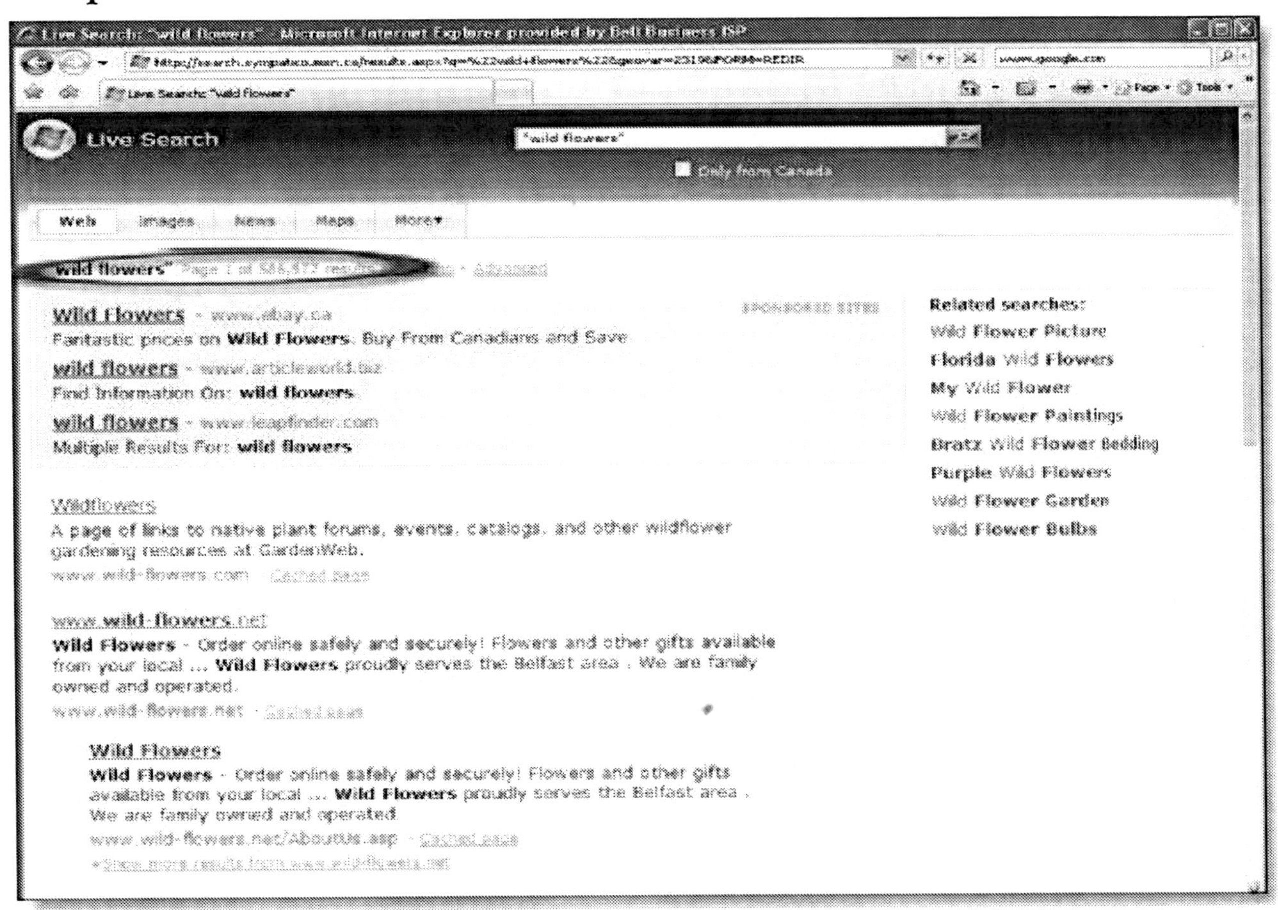

An important difference between msn.com search results and those of the other two main SEs already covered (i.e. google.com, yahoo.com) is that msn.com only lists sponsored paid advertisements directly above the generic ranked results on the left (i.e. the shaded ads at the top left). Instead of listing ads on the right-hand side as the other two SEs do, msn.com lists links to related generic search results.

In contrast to Google.com (1.3 million) and Yahoo.com (1.6 million), the msn.com search returned about 586,000 Web results related to the term "wild flowers".

These differences in number and ranking of results should once more drive home the point made in the previous section that; if you are seriously researching a particular subject it is advisable to repeat the same searches for at least the Big Three search engines: google.com, yahoo.com and msn.com.

Sample Searches – "Images"

For demonstration purposes, let's stick with the "wild flowers" example that was used in the previous section for a "Web" search. The first example below is an "Images" search using Google.com.

Sample Search – "Images" - Google

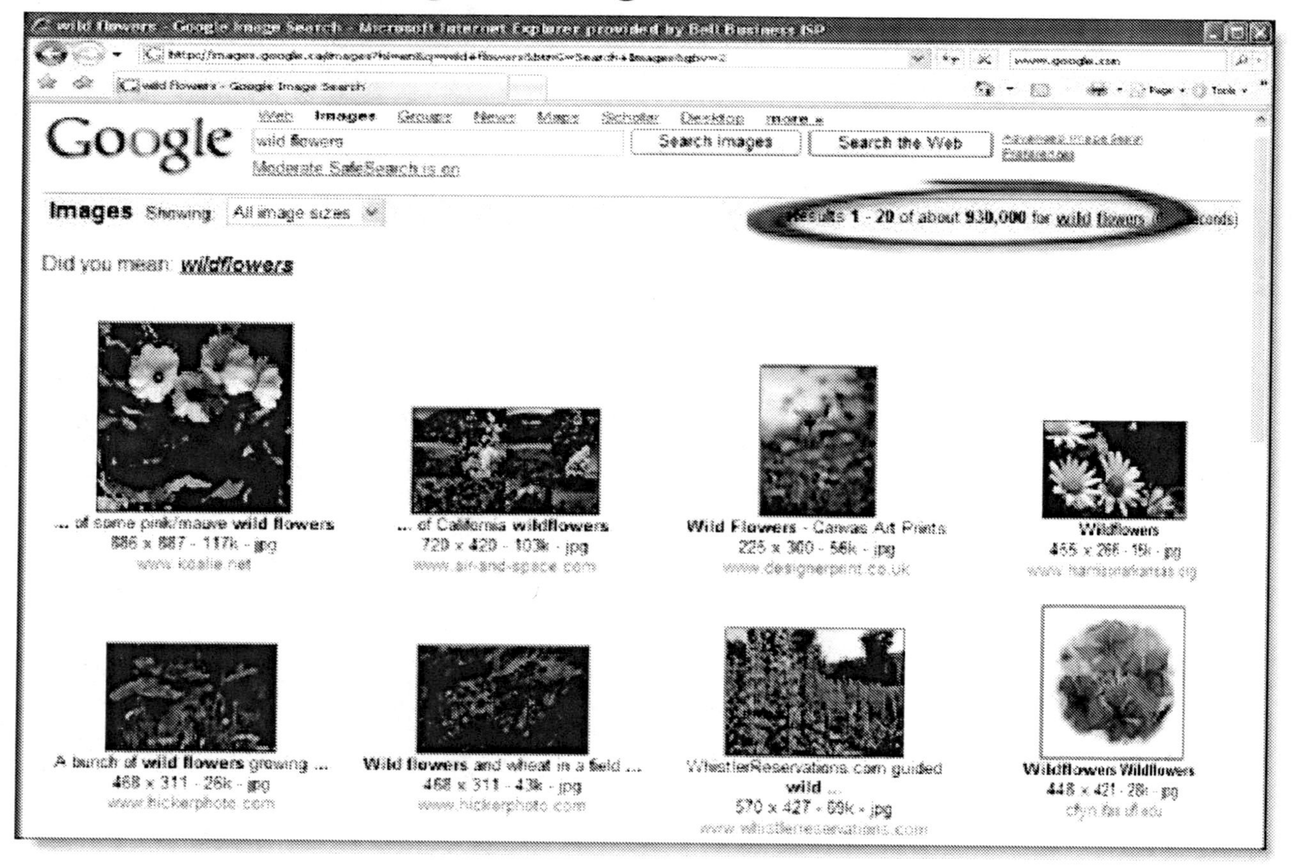

Notice from the "Results" message on the top right of the Results window; Google found 930,000+ images of "wild flowers" on the Web. However, just as noted with the text-based search results shown earlier, as you scroll down through the first few pages of results, the quality and relevancy of those results will diminish rapidly.

TIP: You can Save or Copy any image by right clicking on it and choosing "Save Target As" or "Copy" on the dropdown menu. Be careful though if you plan to use an image for more than your personal non-commercial use; since legally you should request permission to use the image from the copyright holder.

Here's another Images search; this time using the Yahoo.com search engine:

Sample Search – "Images" – Yahoo!

As you can see from the Image Results line in the above screen shot, Yahoo! found more than 165,000 results related to wild flower images. However, when I scrolled down through the results I could see that they were becoming more vague and less relevant by the fifth page I looked at.

Another point to note here is how these results produced by Yahoo! differ significantly from those returned by Google on the pervious page.

This significant difference in number of results found and then the relative ranking of results serves to illustrate once again how search engine results will vary between SEs for exactly the same search term. As mentioned before, this is a direct function of their different proprietary search algorithms (formulas).

Finally, here are the results of that "wild flowers" Image search using msn.com:

Sample Search – "Images" – MSN

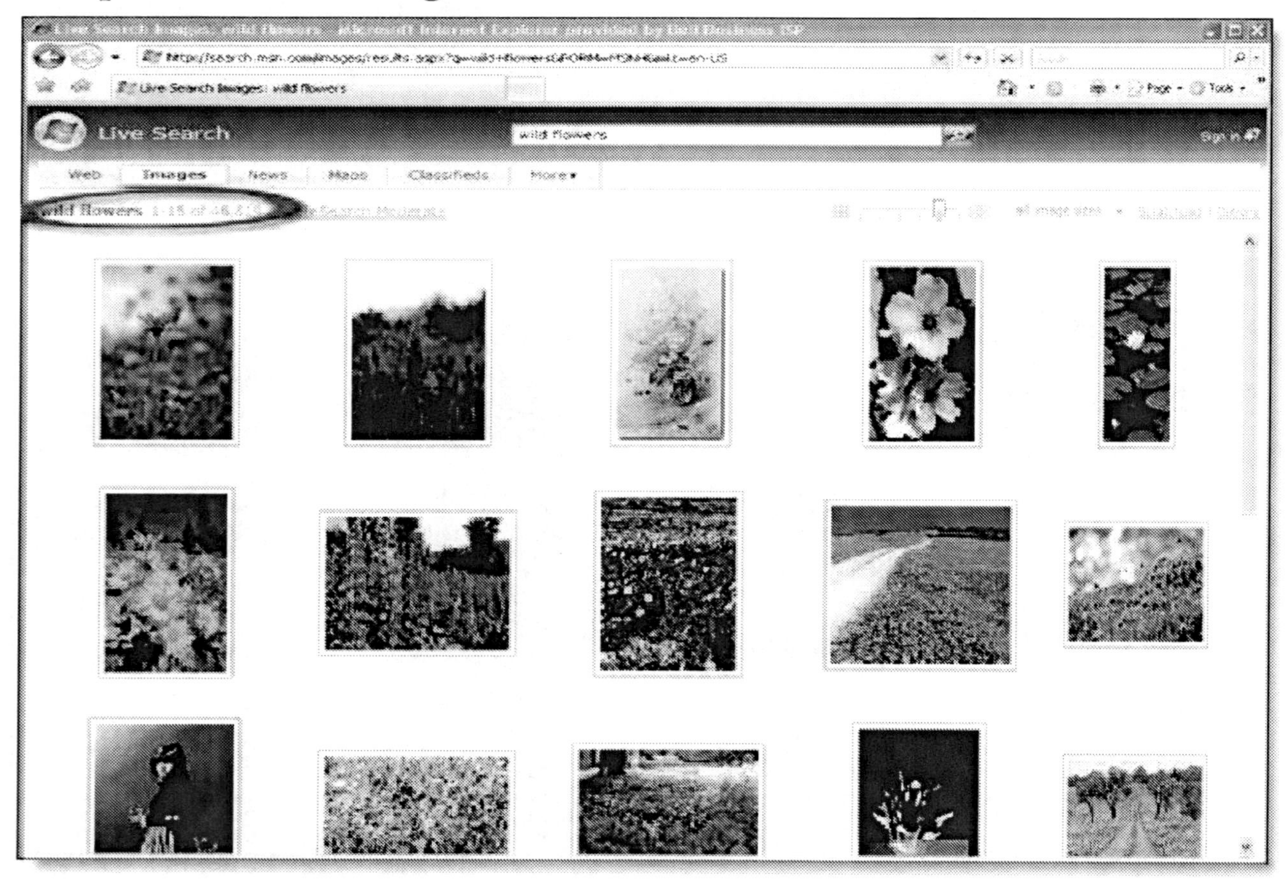

In contrast to Google.com (930,000+) and Yahoo.com (165,000+) the msn.com search returned about 46,000 Image results related to wild flowers.

Once again, the search results for exactly the same term used with the other two main SEs show different results, ranked differently; right from the very first page of results.

This should once more drive home the point made in the previous chapter that if you are seriously researching a particular subject it is advisable to repeat the same searches for at least the Big Three search engines: google.com, yahoo.com and msn.com.

Sample Searches – "News"

Similar to the sample searches of "Images" that are covered in the previous section, I am including a brief section on sample "News" searches below.

To conduct a "News" search in any one of the three main search engines just go to the main search page of the SE and click on "News" just above the search box, as shown on page 114.

For the sake of consistency and easy comparison I am sticking with the "wild flowers" theme for these examples also.

Sample Search – "News" – Google

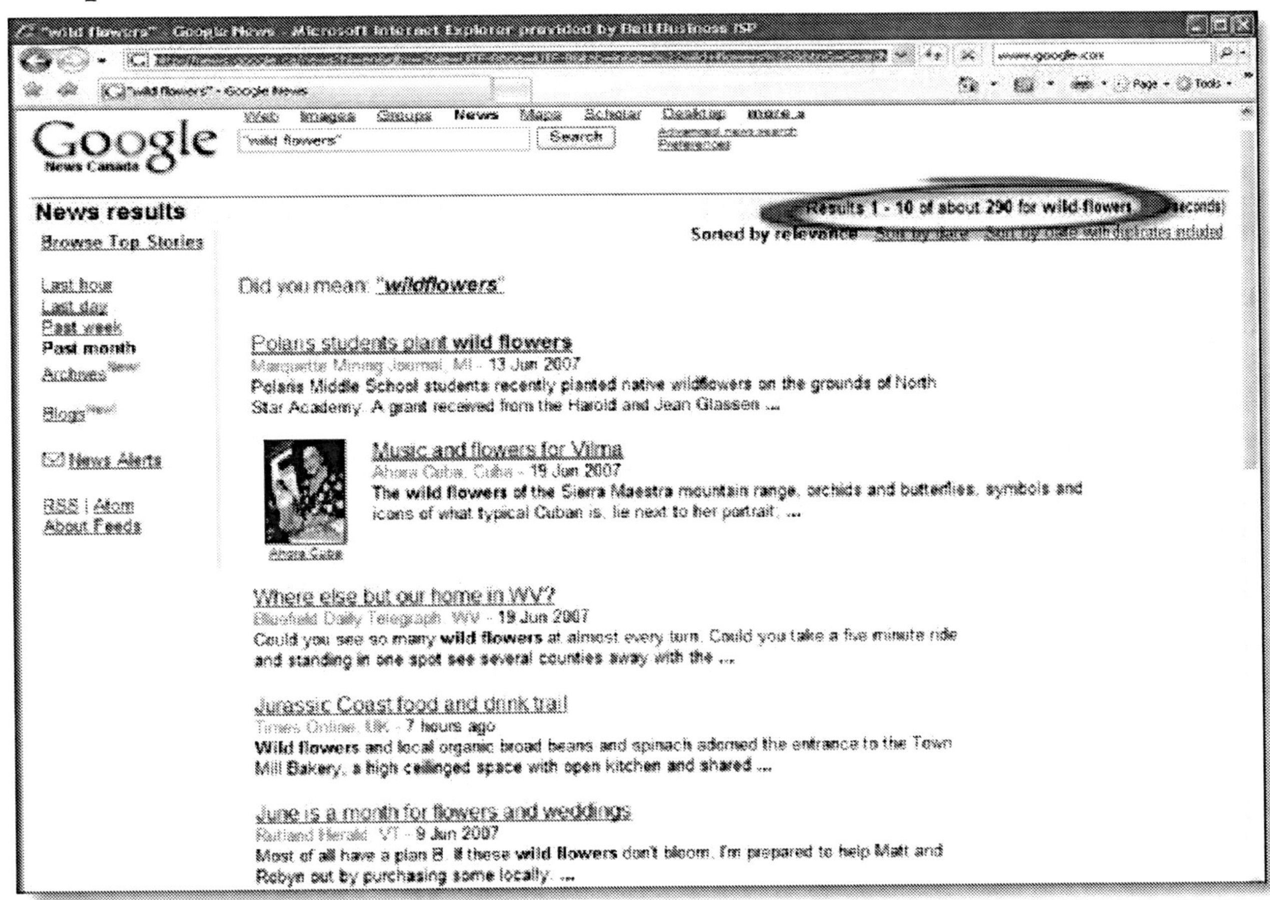

Yes, believe it or not, there is regular news posted online about wild flowers! As you can see above, Google found some 290 relevant results when I did this search.

The following page shows you the results of "News" searches I did at both Yahoo.com and MSN.com.

Sample Search – "News" – Yahoo!

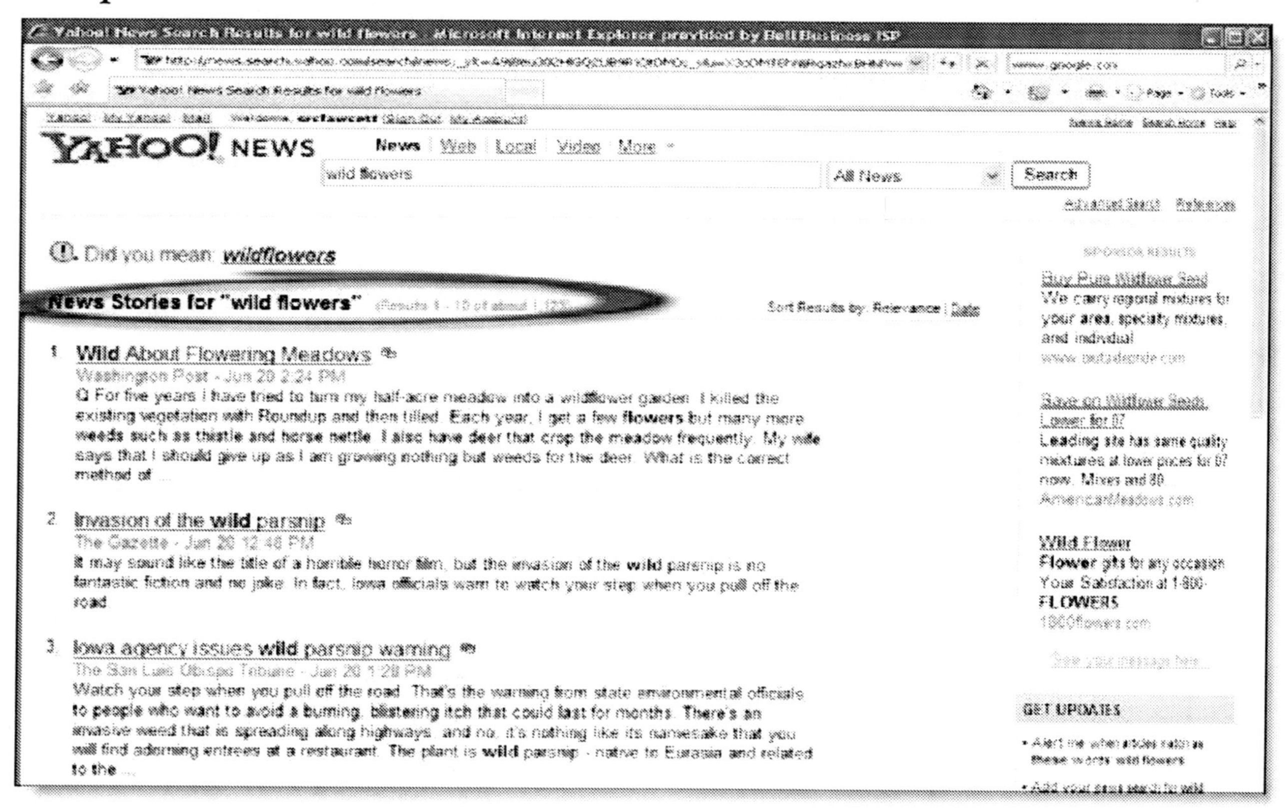

Sample Search – "News" – MSN

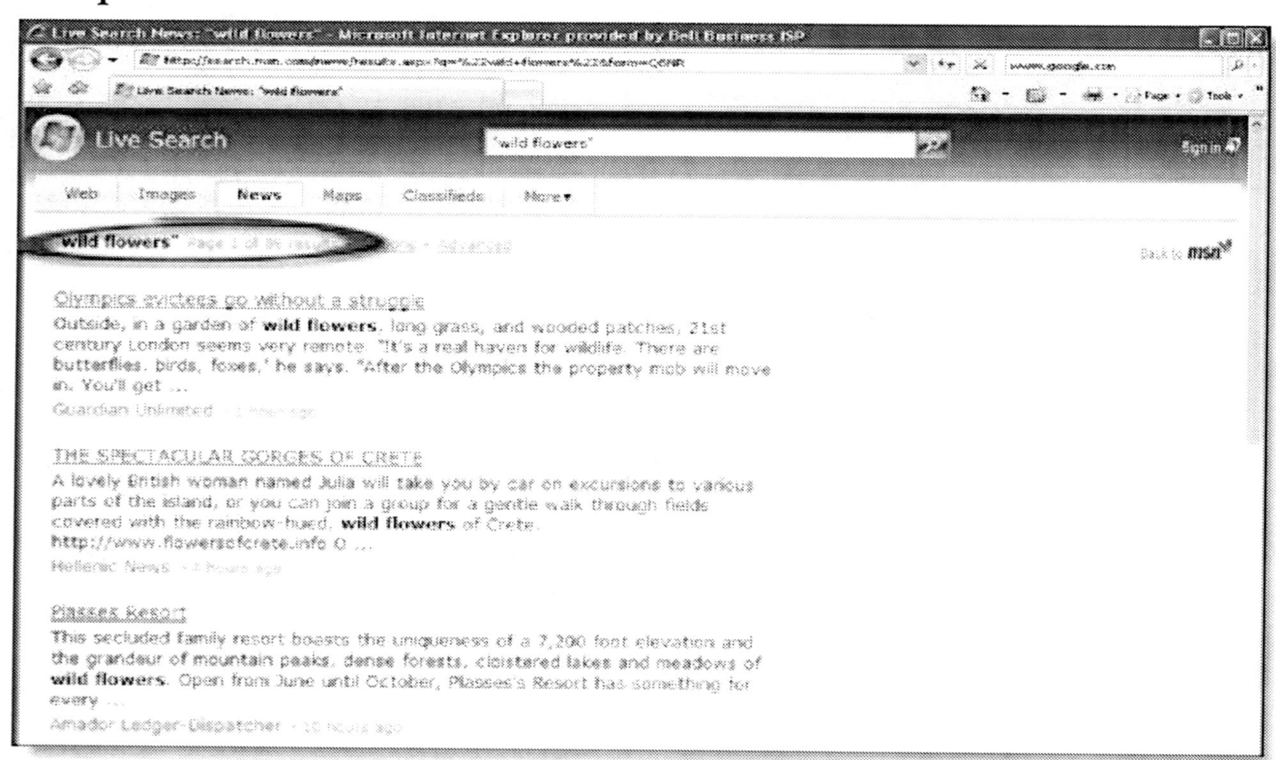

How To Search - Tips and Tricks

Whenever you are searching for anything using a search engine try to be as precise as possible. Search engines are geared to return what they consider to be the "most relevant" results they can find for a search term provided. But, if your search term is too general, your search results may be too general as well.

For example; if you are looking for information on how to write a specific type of letter make sure you specify the exact type of letter in your search term/phrase. So, instead of "letter" or "letter writing" or "how to write a letter", specify "introduction letter" or "how to write introduction letter". Or, if you are looking for sample letters or templates for that type of letter, specify something like "sample introduction letter" or "introduction letter template". Be as specific as you can.

Also, whenever your search term is more than one word, enclose the term in quotes when you enter the search phrase into the search box.

Sticking with the example above, if you enter the two words *introduction letter,* not enclosed in quotes, most search engines will return all results where the words *introduction* and *letter* appear on the same page, but not necessarily together. So for instance a webpage with the phrase; "After the general *introduction* of participants each one was asked to provide a *letter* of recommendation." Although, such a result would appear, it would be irrelevant to a search for how to write an "introduction letter".

By enclosing the search term "introduction letter" in quotes, most search engines will only return results where the exact phrase "introduction letter" is present.

Also, don't forget to try alternative phrasing for your search term/phrase. For example, after searching for "introduction letter", in quotes, I would then search for the phrase "letter of introduction", also enclosed in quotes, since I know that phrase is an alternative term that is widely used.

Bottom Line: The more precise your search terms, the more precise your search results will be.

Typically, when you conduct a search for a term, the SE will return thousands of results ranked in order of relevancy.

What this means is that the highest ranking search results returned are what that particular search engine deems to be the most relevant for the specific search you are conducting -- based on that SE's proprietary (i.e. secret) relevancy formula.

So, you will never get exactly the same search results by conducting the same search on two different search engines. Let's check this out for a minute using our "introduction letter" example at both google.com and yahoo.com.

Google Search Results – "introduction letter"

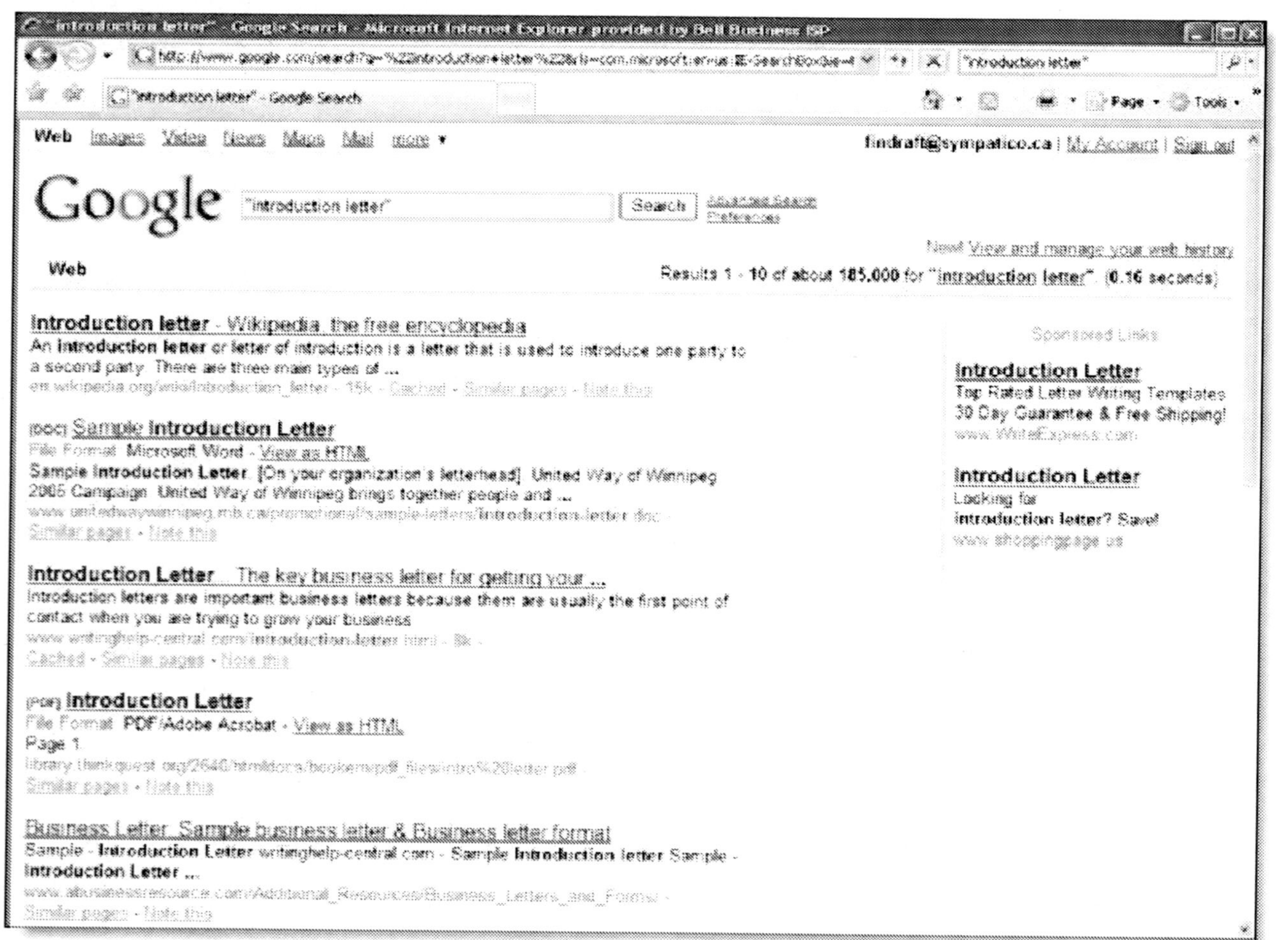

Please note that the results listed on the left-hand side of the results page are the true search results ranked by relevancy. The links listed on the right-hand side of the page for both google and yahoo are paid advertisements. (i.e. Sponsored Links).

Yahoo Search Results – "introduction letter"

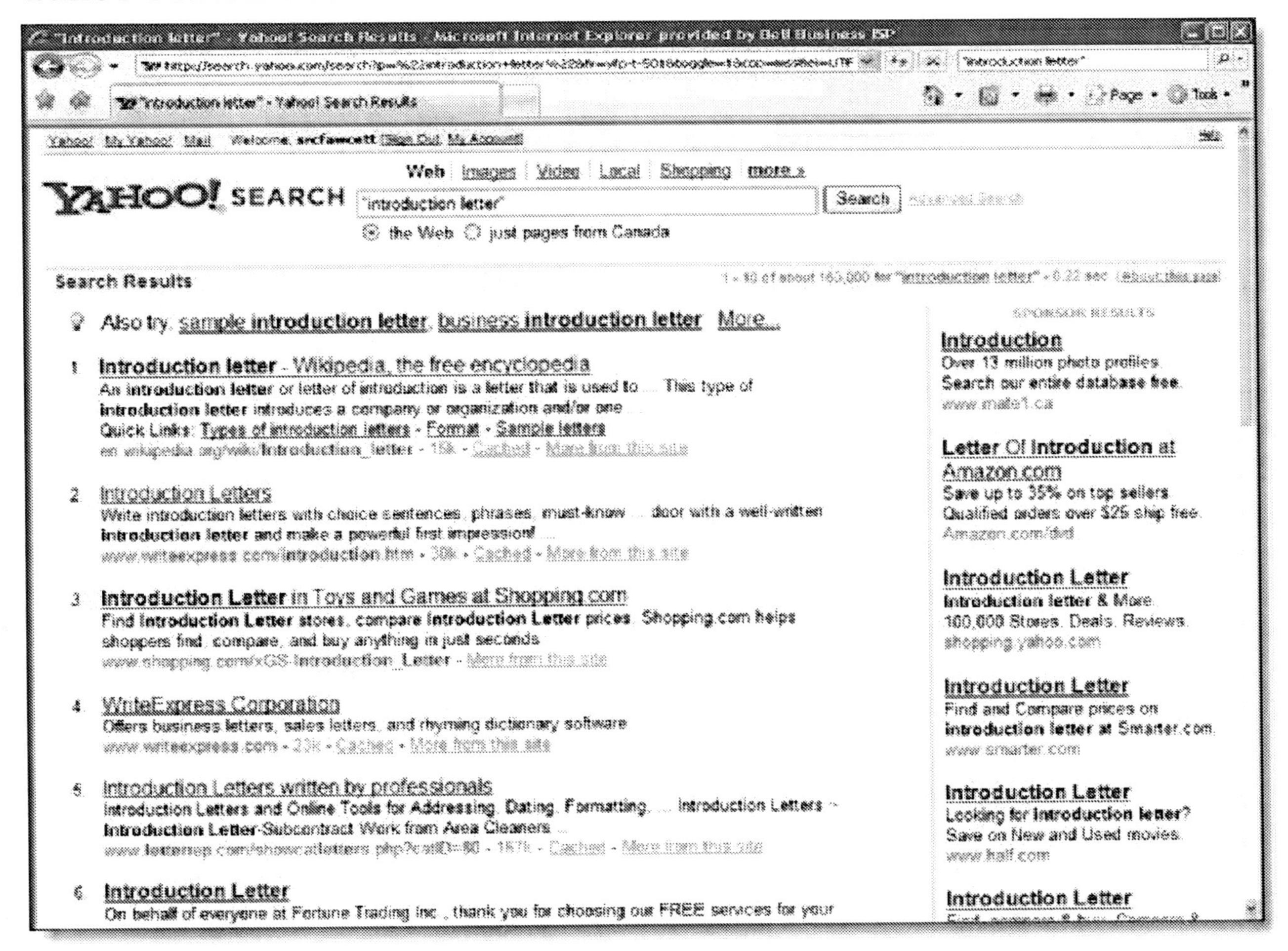

Interestingly, in this particular example both google and yahoo rank the same webpage first. However, after that there are no other matches in the first half-dozen results.

You will also note that google ranked 185,000 pages for that particular search phrase while yahoo ranked 163,000. As I stated above, these results will always vary since both SEs maintain their own databases of pages and use their own ranking formulas.

Something you will notice once you do a few specific searches is that, regardless of the SE used, the results will quickly become less relevant as you scroll through the pages. In fact, I rarely go beyond the first 30 or 40 search results before quality starts to diminish.

A good way to find quality sites related to your search is to go to a few of the most relevant of the sites returned and check the "links" they have posted there.

How To Go Straight To A Destination URL

Searching for websites of interest via a search engine is the most common way that people end up at destination sites. However, another way that people go to particular websites is by entering into their browser a specific URL that they get from an outside source.

For example, people often get URLs of interest from advertisements on radio, television, newspapers, magazines, flyers, etc. They just jot them down or tear them out when they come across them so that they can later check out the website when they are sitting in front of their computer with access to the Internet.

To do this you simply enter that URL directly into the Address/Location Field in your browser toolbar. For example, say we hear about a site called Wikipedia for the first time and we want to check it out. Just open up your browser, type in "www.wikipedia.org", hit the Enter Key, and you will be taken directly to that website.

If there is already something in that field you can highlight it and delete it, or you can just type over it. Just make sure you delete any characters from the previous URL.

As I mentioned earlier, these days you don't even have to type in the entire URL. For instance, typing in "wikipedia.org" in the above case would work just fine.

OTHER USEFUL INFORMATION

In addition to the information contained earlier in this book related directly to sending and receiving e-mails and surfing the Net, this section contains some general "nice to know" information that should be useful to the average beginner.

Common Internet Terms

Here are a few common Internet and Internet-related terms that one will invariably encounter at some point when navigating around the World Wide Web using a personal computer. A number of these terms are covered in more detail in the relevant sections earlier in this book. Deliberately, these are the short, plain-English definitions.

Please take note that this is NOT an exhaustive list of online terms and definitions. It is what I consider to be a representative list of the majority of terms and definitions that the average Internet beginner is likely to come across online and perhaps wonder about.

Baud

This is the unit of measurement used to define the speed at which a modem can transmit and receive data. For example, a 56K modem transfers data at a speed of approximately 56,000 baud.

Blog

Short for the term "Web log", a blog is a website or webpage that is a running log of regular online postings of thoughts, opinions and/or information by the owner. The information posted by the blogmaster is usually focused on a specific theme or niche.

Browser

A software program used to view information on the Internet. The two most popular Browsers right now are Microsoft Internet Explorer and Mozilla Firefox. (See pg. 11).

CD-ROM

This is the predominant portable storage medium for electronic information. It is the same size as a music CD and holds over 600 Mbytes of information. Most software programs come on CD-ROM these days.

Cookies

Cookies are small bits of information about you that some websites you visit store on your computer. The primary reason for them is so that the next time you visit that particular site you won't have to re-enter all of the registration information.

Cyberspace

A popular term used to describe activities related to the "virtual" world of electronic information technology and communications.

Domain Name

A naming convention used on the Internet to uniquely identify the address of organizations and individuals on the Web. For example: www.nytimes.com. See definition for "URL". (See pg. 107).

Download

This is whenever files and or data are transferred electronically from anywhere on the Internet "down" to your computer. The opposite of download is Upload.

E-business

The rapidly growing industry of companies and individuals selling goods and services electronically over the Internet.

E-commerce

The conduct of financial transactions electronically over the Internet such as, buying items and paying for them online by credit card.

Encryption

A method of converting the text of an e-mail into a special code that only the sender and receiver can understand. Used as a security measure to protect privacy.

E-mail

The most frequently used service on the Net whereby users send electronic messages from their computer to anyone else with an Internet e-mail address. (see pg. 21).

FAQ

A common term seen around the Internet that stands for Frequently Asked Questions.

FTP

This stands for File Transport Protocol and is the method that is used to download or upload files on the Internet using what are called FTP servers.

Freeware

Software programs available to Internet users that can be downloaded to a personal computer and used free of charge.

Gigabytes

Gigabytes is one of the most frequently used standard units of measurement for computer storage capacity. These days, the capacity of computer memory and disk storage capacity is usually measured in terms of Gbytes (GB). (See also Mbytes).

Hacker

An expert and often obsessive computer programmer who gains unauthorized access into computer systems, usually with illegal intent. Victims can include large companies, governments, and individuals.

Hard Disk

This is the permanent place (i.e. hardware) on your computer where files are copied to and where you retrieve them from after they have been copied. Usually referred to as "C-drive." Hard disks can store huge amounts of data. (See pg. 9).

Hardware

Any physical piece of equipment that makes up part of your computer system. For example: computer, monitor, modem and printer are all hardware components.

Home Page

The welcome or starting Internet page for any entity with an Internet address. Sometimes also referred to as the "index page" or "landing page".

HTML

Hypertext Markup Language is the programming language used to create electronic pages on the Internet. Also referred to as HTM.

HTTP

Hypertext Transport Protocol is the technical term for the way data files are transferred over the World Wide Web. (See "FTP").

Hyperlink

This is the name for the "links" that let you move from place-to-place within a Web site or from site-to-site on the Web. Links are normally underlined, highlighted in blue, and sprout a little hand when you move the mouse pointer over them. (See pg. 12).

Icon

These are the small graphical symbols that one double clicks their mouse on to initiate the operation of a computer software program. (See pg. 10).

ISP

An Internet Service Provider or ISP is the company or organization that provides you with access to the Internet. It is usually, but not always, a paid service. (See pg. 11).

Mbytes

Megabytes is the standard unit for the measurement of computer storage capacity. The capacity of computer memory and disk storage capacity are always measured in terms of Mbytes (MB). (See also, Gigabytes).

Modem

A device installed in your computer that allows it to send and receive data via telephone lines or coaxial cable. Can be located in a separate box external to your computer.

Netiquette

This term that has been coined to describe appropriate etiquette on the Net, particularly when sending e-mails and conducting other types of online communications. These generally accepted of online behavior have evolved over time. (See pg. 65).

Offline

Refers to when your computer is not connected to the Internet.

Online

The opposite of offline, referring to when your computer is connected to the Internet.

Portal

A website that acts as a "gateway" starting point to access the World Wide Web.

RAM

This stands for Random Access Memory. This is the internal memory of your computer that is used by the various software programs while they are active on your computer.

Search Engine

An Internet website where users can enter keywords to help them find the information and/or sites they are looking for, such as google.com, yahoo.com, etc. (See pg. 109).

Server

These are the larger computers that link the typical Internet user's home computer with the rest of the World Wide Web. (See pg 11).

Shareware

Software that is available for download by Internet users that can normally be used free of charge for a limited trial period, after which one can purchase it for ongoing use.

Site

The destination of a unique Internet address and the place where the "content" for an Internet entity is found. (See Website).

Snail Mail

This term is often used these days to describe regular mail. The obvious inference being that normal mail is very slow compared with e-mail.

Software

This refers to any computer program that runs on your computer. For example; an Operating System such as Windows, your Web Browser program, and your E-Mail program, are all software.

Spam

Unsolicited commercial junk mail sent to your e-mail address without you having given specific permission to the sender to send e-mails to you. (See pg. 61).

Surf

A term used widely to describe the act of a person moving from site-to-site on the Internet via “links” or "hyperlinks". (See pg. 91).

Toolbar

This term describes a grouping of Buttons displayed in the active window of a computer software program, that when clicked or double-clicked by a mouse, activate specific functions of the software. For example, the Toolbar of MS-Explorer appears at the top edges of the active window and contains such functions as Back, Forward, Reload, Home, Search, etc. (See pg. 27).

URL

The unique Uniform Resource Locator address that is assigned to each site on the World Wide Web. They are always prefixed with “www.”. (See “Domain Name”).

Virus

The term used to describe unwanted and destructive computer programs that can seriously damage the software programs that reside on the computers of unsuspecting users. Normally spread by opening suspect e-mail attachments. (See pg 61).

Website

The destination of a www address where all of the electronic pages of an entity’s material are stored. Also referred to as a Site.

Webmail

This is e-mail that is sent, received, and managed using an online Webmail service instead of an e-mail program based on a PC. Examples include Hotmail.com.

Webmaster

This is the individual who is responsible for the design, operation and ongoing maintenance of a Web site.

Wireless

The ability to transmit electronic information from one device to another without the use of wires or cables. Usually requires a special wireless modem.

World Wide Web

Another term for the Internet, and the explanation of the www prefix on all Internet addresses. Also referred to as the Web. (See pg. 12).

WYSIWYG

This commonly used acronym stands for What You See Is What You Get. For example, when something is WYSIWYG it will appear exactly the same in print as it does on your screen.

More Information

For much more detail on many of the above terms you can consult: "Wikipedia, the free online encyclopedia that anyone can edit."
http://wikipedia.org

INDEX

H

I

J

L

M

N

O

NOTES

NOTES

NOTES

Printed in the United States
105147LV00005B/298/A

9 780978 170035